LONGEVITY RULES
HOW TO AGE WELL INTO THE FUTURE

Stuart Greenbaum
Editor

ESKATON.
Senior Residences and Services

866-ESKATON | www.eskaton.org

Eskaton
Public Relations and Brand Management
5105 Manzanita Avenue
Carmichael, CA 95608

916-334-0810 or 866-ESKATON

www.eskaton.org

Contact Eskaton at longevityrules@eskaton.org to purchase a copy of *Longevity Rules* or to inquire about bulk quantity discounts.

Cover and book design by Jere Fass Designs (www.fassdesigns.com)

Senior Residences and Services

About Eskaton:
Eskaton provides community living and home-based support to enhance the independence and quality of living for more than 14,000 older adults annually throughout Northern California. The nonprofit organization's full spectrum of aging services includes residential living with services, assisted living, memory care, hospice, rehabilitation and skilled nursing, home care, adult day healthcare and multiple other special programs and initiatives. Innovation, affordability, collaboration, education and compassion are Eskaton standards as it endeavors to transform the aging experience. Founded in 1968, Eskaton is headquartered in Carmichael, California. Contact Eskaton at 866-ESKATON (866-375-2866) or visit www.eskaton.org for more information.

CONTENTS

Mathematical:

LONGEVITY RULES

Stuart Greenbaum, Editor

Defining "longevity" is easy: long life. Giving context to the word and its implications presents more of a challenge. A challenge that has individuals and society teetering precariously between opportunity and crisis. Will we heed Peter Drucker's advice, "The best way to predict the future is to invent it"? Or will we continue as passive participants in our increasing life expectancy? Not to be overly dramatic, but lives hang in the balance ... figuratively and literally.

Longevity Rules: How to Age Well Into the Future attempts to validate its optimistic title by sharing the insights of 34 of the country's top authorities on longevity. The goal for the whole of this compendium, as much as for the individual essays, is to improve the aging experience by endeavoring to provoke thought, generate dialogue and ultimately persuade action among policyshapers in government, business, public service, healthcare, academics and media.

Stuart Greenbaum is vice president, public relations and brand management for Eskaton, the Northern California-based provider of community living and home-based support for older adults. He is responsible for managing the Eskaton brand and for developing resources to promote a quality aging experience. In his 30-plus years as a public relations counselor, he has produced numerous national and statewide public-service campaigns, two of which earned Emmy Awards. Prior to joining Eskaton in 2009, he served as public relations director for three years with Aging Services of California, where he produced the books *Before the Age Boom Goes ...* and *Media Takes: On Aging*.

Rules. There is no shortage of surveys that profess to define what individuals, particularly the Boomer generation, will want or need in the later years of their aging experience. But something is fundamentally wrong with these surveys and their results. No one knows with any certainty what they will want or need 20 or 30 years in the future. (In fact, most of us often think differently today than we did yesterday or the year before.) It is human nature to reprocess as we gain more information and adjust to new circumstances. To further marginalize the value of many attitudinal studies, consider that for many individuals the denial of aging might be more appropriately qualified as the *delay* of aging. Our journey to "old age" (and eventual frailty and unhealthiness) is inevitable, but it will just take longer to get there than it did for our parents. *Longevity Rules: How to Age Well Into the Future* is the antidote to this preponderance of consensus based on wishful thinking.

The content is divided into three chapters, which are not necessarily intended to be read sequentially. Same goes for the essays. This is a reference guide — ideally which encourages its text to be highlighted, pages to be bookmarked and material to be quoted.

Chapter I: Aging: By the Numbers, prepared by the Boomer Project, synthesizes the most credible, interesting and relevant knowledge about our aging population. It should help to inform and give perspective to the essays that follow.

Chapter II: Context and Commentary is an issue-by-issue attempt to influence public opinion. With respect to longevity, it is an unprecedented approach using nearly three-dozen independent, renowned authorities to accomplish what Edward L. Bernays, the father of modern public relations, referred to as the "engineering of consent." Also unique, this public-interest advocacy features many disparate disciplines and perspectives, including medicine,

gerontology, technology, economics, public policy, demographics, sociology, philosophy, education, communications and aging
services, among others. The sections — Political, Medical, Societal,
Behavioral and Mathematical — generally categorize these essays by
subject matter.

Each author was invited to prepare a 750- to 1,500-word essay
to help place longevity in context; and to present the work as a jour-
nalistic opinion piece — provocative with a distinct "call to action."
Only minimal editing was performed, intentionally to preserve the
integrity of each author's unique contribution. Though some phrases
and words, notably "older adults," are preferred (by this editor), references to seniors, elderly, elders, aged and so forth remain since they
do not change the message. "Boomer" is capitalized throughout; and
"healthcare" is one word. Otherwise, consistency sort of takes a back
seat to individual editorial license.

Chapter III: Reasons to Believe offers hope and promise for
aging well by showcasing more than two-dozen innovative concepts,
models and programs that have successfully anticipated and re-
sponded to older adults' needs and wants. The case studies, gathered
by Harry (Rick) Moody, AARP's director of Academic Affairs, are intended to intrigue and perhaps inspire, thought not necessarily to
endorse without qualification.

About the publisher. Eskaton endeavors to lead by example, to
innovate. The organization's vision statement reads: *Transforming
the Aging Experience.* The 42-year-old nonprofit provides a full
spectrum of community living and home-based support to more
than 14,000 older adults annually throughout Northern California.
Beyond this, The Senior Connection, Livable Design By Eskaton,
Thrill of a Lifetime By Eskaton, Eskaton Celebrates 100+ and other
initiatives distinguish Eskaton as a vital, socially responsible leader

in aging services. *Longevity Rules* exemplifies this commitment to serve the general public (our future consumers) as well as our current residents and program participants. After all, Eskaton is the "Official Sponsor of Longevity."

Acknowledgments. *Longevity Rules* would not have become reality without the early commitment to participate by Dr. Robert Butler, founder and president of the International Longevity Center-USA. (Once you can claim that your team includes the field of longevity's equivalent to Babe Ruth, pretty much everyone wants to play.) Dr. Butler's involvement *independently validated* the authenticity and potential of this project, and no doubt persuaded more than a few renowned authorities to participate. Of course it is these individual authors who graciously shared their time and expertise, without compensation, who are most appreciated.

Matt Thornhill and John Martin with the Boomer Project deserve many thanks for their expert counsel and for their comprehensive, creative contributions.

Special recognition is due AARP's Harry (Rick) Moody, whose advice, resources and editing positively influenced every part of this project.

This monumental project would not have been initiated and completed without the unqualified support of Todd Murch, president and CEO of Eskaton; and the encouragement of Sheri Peifer, vice president, research and strategic planning. Public relations associate Suzanne Strassburg also contributed immensely to the publishing process, while at the same time directing Eskaton's multiple other public relations initiatives.

AGING: BY THE NUMBERS

AGING: BY THE NUMBERS

Boomer Project

E ach generation in living memory has reinvented the final stage of life. The G.I. Generation took an early idea of "retirement" as a way station for people too worn out to work and refashioned it into a two-decade-long span of leisure. Retirement became a reward for a lifetime of labor: a time for activity, travel and security. The G.I.s gave rise to Sun City and other seniors-only communities. They enshrined healthcare for the elderly as a right. They campaigned against stereotypes of the elderly as frail and infirm. They formed advocacy associations for all who joined them in retirement. They even changed the language: "Old people" became "senior citizens."

Members of the Silent Generation have largely accepted the broad outlines of aging bequeathed by the G.I.s but they have changed the style. Grandma has abandoned Mahjong and picked up yoga. Grandpa has dropped the shuffleboard stick and strapped on jogging shoes. Bored by age-segregated communities, many empty-nester Silents are partial to urban condos near restaurants, museums and nightlife where they can mix with young people. Snubbing charter tours on buses, they relish adventure vacations and getaways with the grandkids. Most notably, the Silents rebel against the idea

---

The Boomer Project (www.boomerproject.com) is the nation's leading authority on marketing to today's older Boomer consumer. They provide marketing research and consulting services to a wide range of companies and organizations, including Johnson & Johnson, AARP, Walmart, Lincoln Financial, American Healthcare Association, Home Instead Senior Care and dozens of others.

of passively growing old. They are healthier, more active and, thanks to plastic surgery and Botox, younger looking than any generation before them.

Today, the Baby Boom Generation stands on the edge of retirement. Due to its prodigious size and sense of entitlement, Boomers have transformed American institutions at every stage in their passage through life. And there is every reason to believe they will institute a transformative approach to growing old like what happened when they got their hands on civil rights, the Vietnam war, the sexual revolution, Women's Lib, the work ethic, the pursuit of material gratification, and entrepreneurial risk taking.

Although Boomers once defined the "youth culture," it would be hasty to assume that they will seek the fountain of youth as the Silents have. More likely, Boomers will bring different values and perspectives to the American way of growing old. Boomers, suggest authors William Strauss and Neil Howe in "The Fourth Turning," may do what they have at every step in the maturing process: "Resist it for awhile, then dabble in it, and ultimately glorify it." Boomers, they predict, will embrace growing older and make it their own. "Boomers will establish elegant new insignia of advanced age — flaunting, not avoiding, the natural imprints of time. Rather than trying to impress the young with G.I.-style energy or Silent-style cool, old Boomers will do so with a Zen-like serenity."

That was a bold prediction when Strauss and Howe wrote their book back in 1997. Indeed, it remains bold today, even as the leading edge of Boomers near the age of traditional retirement with the Silent Generation still defining what it means to be old. We are not here to endorse their prophesy, but we bear it in mind as we lay out the numbers that drive the future of aging. We can always count on trends to continue in the same direction — until they change. Unfortunately, the numbers rarely announce in advance when they will launch into new trajectories.

That said, some numbers have considerable momentum behind them. The U.S. Census Bureau projects with considerable confidence that, barring an unprecedented calamity, the number of Americans over the age of 65 will increase over the next 20 years from 40 million in 2010 to more than 70 million in 2020. We can safely say, based on consistent and overwhelming responses to consumer surveys, that Boomers would rather age in place, at home, than in an institutional setting. We also can safely say, based on hard economic numbers, that most Boomers have not saved enough to finance a secure and comfortable retirement. The Center for Retirement Planning at Boston College pegs that figure at just under half of all Boomers. Finally, at the risk of straying into the political realm, we can suggest that the United States will be hard pressed fiscally to honor its commitments to Social Security and Medicare when all the Boomers have passed the 65-year mark.

Logic tells us that there is a considerable gap between Boomer aspirations for their third and fourth quarters of life and what they as individuals, supplemented by the federally-financed social safety net, can afford. The numbers point unmistakably to a future of lessened material expectations for Boomers. What the numbers cannot tell us is how Boomers will respond to that challenge. At the very least, we suspect that Boomers still hold a few surprises in store before they pass into history.

The Boomer Wave

Here's what we can say with reasonable confidence: The next generation of older Americans will live longer, perhaps healthier lives than their predecessors did, and there will be more of them than ever before.

Two forces are driving the rapid aging of the population. The population bulge of graying Boomers is one. The lengthening life expectancy of all Americans is the other. The number of births for each generations show the magnitude of the Boomer bulge:

G.I. Generation	1905-25	50 million
Silent Generation	1926-45	35 million
Boomers	1946-64	76 million
Generation X	1965-82	65 million
Millennials (Gen Y)	1983-02	80 million

In addition to the aging of the Boomer bulge, we must factor in the life expectancy of Americans reaching the age of 65, which increases several months with the passage of every decade.

Boomers plus longer life expectancies mean that the number of Americans over 60 will increase by 70 percent by 2025, according to AARP's "Boomers: The Next 20 Years Map of Future Landscape Affecting Boomers." The increase in the older adult population will account for the vast bulk of growth in the American population as a whole, making them the demographically dominant sector of society.

U.S. POPULATION CHANGE, 2005-2025

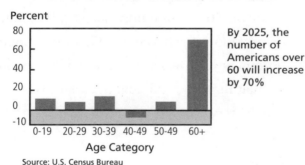

By 2025, the number of Americans over 60 will increase by 70%

Source: U.S. Census Bureau

The most pronounced increase will occur in the oldest old category of people 85 years and older, an age group that historically requires exceptionally high levels of caregiving and medical treatment.

PROJECTED POPULATION 85+

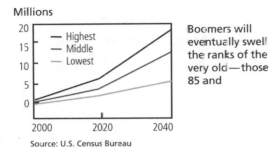

Millions

Legend:
— Highest
— Middle
— Lowest

2000   2020   2040

Boomers will eventually swell the ranks of the very old—those 85 and

Source: U.S. Census Bureau

There are no surprises in these numbers. They are well-known. In fact, Americans have had half a century to prepare for the age wave. It is a shame we are not more ready for it now that it is here.

Good News, Bad News: Longevity and Chronic Illness

The gift of long life may be the greatest blessing of modern society. But it comes with a caveat. While a long, *healthy* life is devoutly to be hoped for, a long life of illness, disability and dependency may be a curse.

It is unfortunate but it is so: If people survive the acute illnesses that killed off much of the population in the past, they contract the chronic illnesses that accompany old age. Longer life expectancies translate into a larger population of Americans with chronic medical conditions. Indeed, according to "Chronic Care: A Call to Action for Health Reform," a March 2009 AARP study, more than 70 million Americans ages 50 and older suffer from at least one chronic condition such as arthritis, osteoporosis, asthma, cancer, heart disease, depression and diabetes.

Eleven million Americans, mostly older adults, live with five or more chronic conditions. The incidence of disability will increase with the advancing age of the population in any case, but the problem is aggravated in the United States by the epidemic of obesity, a contributor to diabetes, heart disease, back problems and other maladies. Between 1997 and 2006, the prevalence of diabetes among adults ages 65 and older increased by more than 50 percent. And a recent study, published in *Diabetes Care* by Elbert S. Huang, projects that between 2009 and 2034, the number of Americans treated for diabetes under Medicare will leap from 8.2 million to 14.6 million — an increase of 78 percent.

Advancing age also engenders a higher rate of disability. "The prevalence of having one or more physical limitations increases with advancing age," conclude the authors of "Aging Differently: Physical Limitations Among Adults Aged 50 Years and Over: United States, 2001-2007." More than 40 percent of adults ages 80 and over have physical limitations; more than 25 percent have three or more physical limitations.

Disabilities range from hearing and vision impairment to difficulty walking, climbing steps, bending over and performing other Activities of Daily Living (ADL). The inability to drive, walk, shop and run errands severely restricts an individual's ability to live independently.

INCIDENCE OF DISABILITIES AMONG OLDER ADULTS

Disability	55+	85+
Hearing impairment	31.6%	62.1%
Vision impairment	11.7%	26.9%
No teeth	19.0%	35.6%
Difficulty walking one mile	25.0%	56.1%
Difficulty walking up 10 steps	20.0%	45.2%
Difficulty stooping or bending	30.3%	53.1%
Difficulty shopping	13.3%	34.1%

Source: "Health Characteristics of Adults Aged 55 Years and Over: United States, 2004-2007"

Older Americans also suffer cognitive disabilities. Perhaps the most devastating is Alzheimer's disease, the risk for which increases in lockstep with advancing age. Currently, according to

"2009 Alzheimer's Disease Facts and Figures," an estimated 5.3 million Americans have Alzheimer's disease — one in eight people 65 and older.

As the number of Americans surviving into their 80s and 90s grows, the incidence of Alzheimer's and other forms of dementia will increase rapidly, too. In 2000, there were an estimated 411,000 new cases of Alzheimer's disease reported. When the Boomers begin reaching their 80s, the number is expected to hit 615,000 a year. The number of new cases could peak around 960,000 a year in 2050.

Until very recently, gerontologists thought there was a silver lining to these gloomy numbers. In a phenomenon they called the "compression of morbidity," the current cohort of older Americans are suffering lower rates of morbidity — fewer disabilities — than did previous generations at comparable ages. On average, older adults were living longer without experiencing a significant loss of independence. But that favorable trend appears to have been thrown into reverse. Boomers are experiencing *more* disabilities than previous generations did at the same age, a study funded by the National Institute on Aging has found.

Among people 80 and older, the data from two national health and nutrition surveys showed improvements for people 80 and older. But there was no change in disability rates among people in their 70s, and disability rates rose among people in their 60s. Lead author Teresa E. Seeman, a UCLA medical school professor, said that higher disability rates appeared to be linked to higher incidence of obesity. "The data ... certainly suggests the baby boomers, whatever health benefits they've enjoyed up until now, may not enjoy such a rosy older age."

While Americans are living longer than ever, the scary implication of the most recent research is that their capacity for independent living may be slipping. As they battle with obesity and the maladies that stem from it, Boomers will experience more chronic conditions and more disabilities than members of the Silent Generation. The impact on healthcare costs will be debilitating. Neither society, much less the Boomers themselves, are financially prepared to deal with it.

Who Will Pay for Old Age?
Boomers are ill-prepared for the financial perils of growing old. Even before the 2008 financial meltdown, it was evident that Boomers were failing to save enough money to maintain their pre-retirement living standards, much less offset the financial risk of living into their 80s and 90s, ages associated with increased chronic illness, disability, and higher payouts for medical and long-term care.

Boomers earned more money at every age than previous generations. But they were record spenders and borrowers as well, driving consumption to fuel more than 78 percent of the growth in Gross Domestic Product vs. 64 percent two decades earlier, according to a June 2008 report by McKinsey & Co., "Talkin' 'bout my generation: The economic impact of aging U.S. Baby Boomers." But they saved only a fraction of their income that previous generations had, relying upon soaring home prices to increase their net worth. Consequently, Boomers were hammered by the collapse in housing prices, then clobbered again by the dive in stock market values. By McKinsey's reckoning, only 38 percent had saved enough to be prepared for retirement.

David Rosnick and Dean Baker painted an even gloomier picture in their February 2009 study, "The Wealth of the Baby Boom Cohorts After the Collapse of the Housing Bubble." They calculated that the median household with a person between the ages of 45 to 54 saw its net worth plummet more than 45 percent between 2004 and 2009, to just $94,200. The loss to early Boomers, between 55 and 64, was even worse: almost 50 percent to $159,800. "The loss of wealth," they conclude, "will make baby boomers far more dependent on Social Security and Medicare than prior generations."

As 2009 unfolded, the prognosis for Boomer retirement got worse. In "Long-term Care Costs and the National Retirement Risk Index," published in March 2009, Alicia H. Munnell and her co-authors suggested that if the soaring costs of healthcare and long-term care were taken into account, the percentage of Boomer and Generation X households "at risk" of having an under-funded retirement approached 64 percent.

Recent data suggests that Boomers are saving more, but they have only a few years to make up a lifetime of neglect. If, as Rosnick and Baker suggest, Boomers are more dependent upon Social Security and Medicare than previous generations, the solvency of Social Security and Medicare becomes a paramount issue.

The outlook for the government-financed social safety net is not a happy one. Given current trajectories, the tax *shortfall* for Social Security and Medicare will increase from less than 2 percent of GDP to more than 7 percent over the next 30 years, according to the 2009 report of the Social Security and Medicare Boards of Trustees.

While there is sufficient money in the Social Security trust fund (OASDI) to keep up payments through 2037, barring any changes to the way the program is structured, Medicare's Hospital trust fund (HI) is projected to run out in 2017 — a date now visible on the horizon. It is an open question whether the federal government will be in a position to make up the difference through general tax revenues, given the fact that the national debt, which now runs around $12 trillion, is expected under an optimistic set of assumptions to be accumulating at the rate of $1 trillion yearly by then.

Boomers then will confront an awful choice: Will they, with their scrawny nest eggs, turn to the government to deliver the same level of retirement security that it provided the G.I.s and Silents before them, whatever the cost to the rest of society? Or will they adapt — will they make do with less? Will they, as Strauss and Howe predict, "find new ethical purpose in low consumption because, with America in crisis, they will have no other choice?"

Who Will Provide the Care?

Just as Boomers spent money and racked up debt with little thought to providing for their winter years, they reshaped the family structure with little thought to the consequences for when they grew old. Just as Boomers face a fiscal/financial crisis, they also face a caregiving crisis.

Spouses and children account for most caregiving for the elderly. Family fills in when seniors find themselves in that awkward stage between full independence and total incapacity. But Boomers will have fewer family members to turn to than their parents did.

As a group, 94 percent of the G.I. and Silent generations got married. Today, among those still with us, 64 percent still have a spouse. Moreover, they have loads of adult children — they're called Boomers. That means most members of the older generations today have spouses to turn to and roughly four children on average to lean on. Boomers, on the other hand, have exponentially fewer family options. Only 87 percent of Boomers got married in the first place, and more of them got divorced. Today one in three Boomers is without a spouse or partner. Also, Boomers had, on average, only two children.

Gerontologist Ken Dychtwald calls it the "Caregiver Crunch." More like a catastrophe, if you ask us.

It is possible to substitute family caregiving with commercial services. But such relationships are less rewarding emotionally, and the care provided by "visiting angels" comes with a price tag. That will pose a major problem for Boomers whose finances, as we have seen, will be stretched to the breaking point. The caregiver problem will be especially acute for Boomer women, who are less likely to have accumulated assets and pension wealth and who are more likely to have outlived their spouse. (Advancing age won't be a day at the beach for older men either: Men are less likely to form supportive social networks than women.)

There's another important dimension to the looming caregiving crisis — the difficulty that Boomers will have maintaining their independence in a largely suburban nation. As the Brookings Institution wrote in its report, "Getting Current: Recent Demographic Trends in Metropolitan America," Boomers are the first suburban generation. "The aging in place of suburban Boomers will ... make the suburbs in most parts of the country a lot grayer than they ever have been before." Most suburban communities cater to the needs of younger populations and families with children. Coping with a wave of older Boomers is a challenge that few are equipped to deal with.

One of the most pressing problems for older adults trying to maintain independence is the auto-centric development pattern of suburban communities. Most streets are designed with the goal of moving automobiles as efficiently as possible, not people on foot or in wheelchairs. A poll conducted by the AARP Public Policy Institute and allied groups and published in "Planning Complete Streets for an Aging America" found that 40 percent of adults 50 and older report inadequate sidewalks in their neighborhoods, while 50 percent said they cannot cross main roads close to their home safely. "The human cost of this is significant," warns AARP. "It exacerbates the social and physical isolation of non-drivers, not to mention the dangers imposed upon all road users."

Technology may be a partial palliative to isolated seniors living alone. In a survey of adults 65 and over, AARP Knowledge Management found that 87 percent preferred to have care delivered to them in their current home, and a similar percentage said they would be willing to give up some of their privacy — mainly to monitors — in order to accomplish that goal. Half were aware how computers could help them maintain social connections, and three-quarters were interested in telemedicine as an alternative to visiting the doctor's office. But today's older adults resisted the use of some technologies. Whether Boomers prove to be as resistant remains to be seen.

Changes in Attitudes

Boomers are the first generation to approach age 65 — leading-edge Boomers will get there in 2011 — and know with some degree of confidence they will live another thirty years, maybe more. With so much time ahead of them, Boomers are redefining what it means to be "old." In a recent study we conducted, Boomers said that middle age starts at age 48 on average, while "old age" doesn't begin until 73 — eight years past the traditional retirement age.

Boomers also are acutely aware that they have not accumulated enough money to live the active lifestyles they've enjoyed most of their life, much less to age in place or protect themselves over 18 years on average from the risk of runaway medical expenses and long-term care. While wrestling with financial anxieties, they also are redefining what they want out of the final phase of life.

The 2008 recession, the worst economic downturn since the Great Depression, sparked a major reappraisal by Americans of all

generations of their fundamental values. In March 2009, the third annual "MetLife Study of the American Dream" found that Americans
regarded the recession as a "wake up call" to abandon the "insatiable
hunger" for more material possessions. Nearly half of all consumers
had concluded they already had all the possessions they needed, up
13 percentage points from the previous poll. Four in 10 Americans
felt "buyer's remorse" about past purchases.

What, then, do Americans value now? In May 2009, Harris
Interactive and Ken Dychtwald released a study, "Retirement at the
Tipping Point," that crystallized the new zeitgeist. Fifty-eight percent
of Americans ranked "success" as "having loving friends and family,"
followed by "the freedom to do what I want" (37 percent), "achieving
financial independence" (33 percent), and "being true to myself and
not selling out" (19 percent). "Having power and influence" logged
in at 3 percent. Boomer attitudes did not differ materially from those
of other generations — but Boomers will be the first to apply the new
values to re-thinking retirement and old age.

Boomers will approach the challenges ahead through their
unique generational lens. The defining generational characteristics
of Boomers can be summarized as follows:

- **Entitlement and personal gratification** — These traits, imbued
  in early childhood and reinforced by decades of affluence, contributed to Boomers becoming world-class consumers. Their
  buying power warped the entire global economy. Their final
  years will be very different. Will they insist that other generations
  make them whole through Social Security and Medicare, or will
  they lead the return to frugality? That's the big question.

- **Control** — Boomers have spearheaded social change for the past
  half century, and they like being in charge. Boomers are not likely
  to accept a top-down, one-size-fits-all solution to the challenges

of aging. Any new institutions they create are likely to be built from the bottom up.

- **Optimism** — Boomers are an up-beat, can-do generation. They view the future optimistically, always seeing the glass as half-full. That may explain why, despite the dire predicament they face in old age, they haven't yet begun to panic.

- **Anti-status quo** — Boomers have been a revolutionary force in American society, continually pushing against the political and business establishment. They are not likely to accept the institutions and practices of aging as handed down by the Silent Generation. If they don't like something, they will push for change.

In our own Boomer Project research on how Boomers are approaching their advancing years, we have described the animating principle as the quest for vitality. Not the fountain of youth, but the fountain of vitality. Boomers don't want to be young again but they do want to slow the downward slide toward frailty and dependence. Boomers want to maintain their physical fitness and mental acuity. They want to maintain active social lives. And, as they get closer to the final passage, death, they want to explore the spiritual dimensions of existence, whether through organized religion or personal quest.

The Boomer cluster of attributes will be tested first in how the generation approaches the first great challenge associated with "old age" — when to retire. Prodded by the collapse in their net worth, Boomers have resolved to work longer before pocketing the gold watch.

Since World War II, if not before, the great ambition of most Americans was to retire at the earliest possible age to enjoy a life of leisure. Year after year, the average retirement age crept lower. In 1950, the average retirement age was 70. By 1990, it had bottomed out at 62. In the past few years, it has started moving back up.

"Work harder, work longer — that appears to be the new motto for older Americans," writes the Pew Research Center in a September 2009 report, "America's Changing Workforce: Recession Turns a Graying Office Grayer." Boomers show a greater inclination than previous generations to stay active longer in the labor market. For people ages 55 to 64, the labor force participation rate increased from 57.2 percent in 1995 to 65.3 percent in early 2009. For people ages 65 and older, the rate increased from 12 percent in 2005 to 17.3 percent in 2009.

There is evidence that the commitment to work longer is a Boomer-related phenomenon, not one that applies equally to all generations. Fifty-two percent of respondents in the 50- to 64-year-old bracket said they had thought about delaying retirement, and some 16 percent said they would never retire, according to "The Threshold Generation," a Pew study released in May 2009. Both numbers were significantly higher than for younger age groups.

The numbers confirm that the Boomers will carry their strong work ethic, one of their most notable generational traits, past the official 65-year-old retirement marker.

The Road Forward

All of these numbers tell us one thing is certain about the future of aging: in many ways, Boomers will do it differently. But how?

We see two options ahead for Boomers. One is for Boomers to transform everything about aging in our society. The other is to transform themselves and their own expectations about growing older. The first is externally focused and the second is internal.

The chance to change the world of aging is significant for Boomers, who have both the size and motivation to do it. In his 2009 book *The Making of an Elder Culture*, Theodore Roszak (a contributor to this book, incidentally) sees Boomers focusing on this external goal: re-turning to the crusading idealism of their youth. Older Boomers will spurn consumerism. They will crusade to improve the environment, fight for social justice and finish the causes they had begun in their youth. "The final stage of life is uniquely suited to the creation of new social forms and cultural possibilities," he writes. "Age offers us the opportunity to detach from the competitive, high-consumption pri-orities that dominated us on the job and in the marketplace."

The second option to change internally is best described by Strauss and Howe, who see a different future for the Boomers. Instead of refighting the battles of their youth, Boomers will turn inward, constructing a new social ethic of decline and death, much as they did in youth with sex and procreation. "Where their youthful ethos hinged on self-indulgence, their elder ethos will hinge on self-denial. As they experience their own bodies coping naturally with decline and death, they will expect government to do the same. ... With the same psychic energy with which they once probed *eros*, Boomers will now explore *thanatos*, the end-time."

Our analysis of monthly consumer surveys by BIGresearch sug-gests that Boomers *are* turning their back on consumerism. They are rediscovering the traditional values of thrift and frugality, which they see as consistent also with emerging "green" values of conservation and recycling.

But whether Boomers will pick up the social causes they fought for a half century ago or turn inward in the search for spiritual fulfill-ment, well, the numbers don't exist. In fact, even if we polled all 76 million Boomers, we would likely get 76 million different responses. In the end, we will have to wait to find out.

Meanwhile, we can gain authoritative insights from the contribu-tors to this book. Think of this as the starting point for the "new rules" for growing old.

Sources

- Summary of the 2009 Annual Reports
  Social Security and Medicare Boards of Trustees
  http://www.ssa.gov/

- "By 2028, Boomers will be most thankful for friends"
  Matt Thornhill
  Richmond Times-Dispatch (November 27, 2009)

- "Why Population Aging Matters: A Global Perspective"
  National Institute on Aging, National Institutes of Health, U.S. Department of Health and
  Human Services, U.S. Department of State
  http://www.nia.nih.gov

- "Getting Current: Recent Demographic Trends in Metropolitan America"
  The Brookings Institution
  William H. Frey, Alan Berube, Audrey Singer, Jill H. Wilson (2009)
  http://www.brookings.edu

- "Planning Complete Streets for an Aging America"
  AARP Public Policy Institute, Renaissance Planning Group, National Complete Streets
  Coalition, Institute of Transportation Engineers (May 2009)
  http://www.aarp.org

- *Healthy @ Home*
  Linda L. Barrett
  AARP Knowledge Management (2008)
  http://www.aarp.org

- "2009 MetLife Study of the American Dream"
  MetLife (March 2009)
  http://www.metlife.com

- "Retirement at the Tipping Point"
  Ken Dychtwald, Harris Interactive (May 2009)
  http://www.agewave.com

- "What a Long, Strange Trip It's Been—And Continues to Be"
  Matt Thornhill
  Richmond Times-Dispatch (November 1, 2007)

- "Sun Life Financial Unretirement Index"
  http://www.sunlife.com

- "The Coming Entrepreneurship Boom"
  Dane Stangler
  Ewing Marion Kauffman Foundation (June 2009)
  http://www.kauffman.org

- "America's Changing Workforce: Recession Turns a Graying Office Grayer"
  Pew Research Center (September 3, 2009)
  http://pewsocialtrends.org

- "The Threshold Generation"
  Rich Morin
  Pew Research Center (May 28, 2009)
  http://pewresearch.org

- *Boomer Consumer: Ten New Rules for Marketing to America's Largest, Wealthiest and
  Most Influential Group*
  Matt Thornhill and John Martin
  Linx Publishing (July 2007)

- *The Making of an Elder Culture*
  Theodore Roszak
  New Society Publishers (September 2009)

CONTEXT AND COMMENTARY

POLITICAL

PURSUIT OF THE 'LONGEVITY DIVIDEND'

Robert N. Butler, M.D.

Imagine an intervention, such as a pill, that could significantly reduce your risk of cancer. Imagine an intervention that could reduce your risk of stroke or dementia or arthritis. Now, imagine an intervention that does all these things, and at the same time reduces your risk of everything else undesirable about growing older: including heart disease, diabetes, Alzheimer's and Parkinson's disease, hip fractures, osteoporosis, sensory impairments and sexual dysfunction. Such a pill may sound like fantasy, but aging interventions already do this in animal models. And many scientists believe that such an intervention is a realistically achievable goal for people. Slow aging should begin immediately — because it will save and expand lives, improve health, and create wealth. The belief that aging is an immutable process, programmed by evolution, is now known to be wrong. Nations may be tempted to continue attacking diseases and disabilities of old age separately, as if they were unrelated to one another. This is the way most medicine is conducted today.

In addition to the obvious health benefits, enormous economic benefits would accrue from the extension of healthy life. By extending the time in the lifespan when higher levels of physical and mental

Robert N. Butler, M.D., is president and CEO of the International Longevity Center. A physician, gerontologist, psychiatrist and public servant, he also is the author of *Why Survive*, for which he won the Pulitzer Prize, and *The Longevity Revolution*. In 1975, he became founding director of the National Institute on Aging of the National Institutes of Health, and in 1982 he founded the first department of geriatrics in a U.S. medical school at The Mount Sinai Medical Center.

capacity are expressed, people would remain in the labor force longer, personal income and savings would increase, age-entitlement programs would face less pressure from shifting demographics, and there is reason to believe that national economies would flourish. The science of aging has the potential to produce what I and others refer to as a "Longevity Dividend" in the form of social, economic and health bonuses both for individuals and entire populations — dividend that would begin with generations currently alive and continue for all that follow. We contend that conditions are ripe today for the aggressive pursuit of the Longevity Dividend by seeking the technical means to intervene in the biological processes of aging in our species, and by ensuring that the resulting interventions become widely available.

According to studies undertaken at the International Longevity Center and at universities around the world, the extension of healthy life creates wealth for individuals who accumulate more savings and investments than those beset by illness. They tend to remain productively engaged in society. They spark economic booms in so-called mature markets, including financial services, travel, hospitality and intergenerational transfers to younger generations. Improved health status also leads to less absenteeism from school and work and is associated with better education and higher income.

Genes that slow growth in early life — such as those that produce differences between large, middle-size and miniature dogs — typically postpone all the signs and symptoms of aging in parallel. A similar set of hormonal signals — related in sequence and action to human insulin, insulin-like growth factor (IGF-I) or both — are involved in aging, life span and protection against injury in worms, flies and mice, and extend lifespan in all of those animals. These hormones help individual cells to buffer the toxic effects of free radicals, radiation damage, environmental toxins and protein aggregates that contribute to various late-life malfunctions. An extension of disease-free lifespan of approximately 40 percent has already been achieved repeatedly in experiments with mice and rats.

If we succeed in slowing aging by seven years, the age-specific risk of death, frailty and disability will be reduced by approximately half at every age. People who reach the age of 50 in the future would have the health profile and disease risk of today's 43-year-olds; those aged 60 would resemble current 53-year-olds, and so on.

The National Institutes of Health is funded at $28 billion in 2009, but less than 0.1 percent of that amount goes to understanding the biology of aging and how it predisposes us to a suite of costly diseases and disorders expressed at later ages. We are calling on Congress to invest $3 billion annually to this effort, or about 1 percent of the 2005 Medicare budget of $309 billion, and to provide the organizational and intellectual infrastructure and other related resources to make this work.

If we succeed in slowing aging by seven years, the age-specific risk of death, frailty and disability will be reduced by approximately half at every age.

Specifically, we recommend that one-third of this budget ($1 billion) be devoted to the basic biology of aging with a focus on genomics and regenerative medicine as they relate to longevity science. Another third should be devoted to age-related diseases as part of a coordinated trans-NIH effort. One-sixth ($500 million) should be devoted to clinical trials with proportionate representation of older persons (aged 65+) that include head-to-head studies of drugs or interventions including lifestyle comparisons, cost-effectiveness studies and the development of a national system for postmarketing surveillance. The remaining $500 million should go to a national preventive medicine research initiative that would include studies of safety and health in the home and workplace, and address issues of physical inactivity and obesity as well as genetic and other early-life pathological influences. This last category would include studies of the social and economic means to affect positive changes in health behaviors in the face of current health crises — obesity and diabetes — that can lower life expectancy. Elements of the budget could be phased in over time, and it would be appropriate to use funds within each category for research, training and the development of appropriate infrastructure. We also strongly encourage the development of an international consortium devoted to this task, as all nations would benefit from securing the Longevity Dividend.

CAN INTERGENERATIONAL CONFLICT BE AVOIDED?

Robert H. Binstock

D uring the past two decades, various politicians, policy pundits, academics and journalists have been predicting that intergenerational political conflict will emerge over the costs of Social Security and Medicare benefits as aging Boomers swell the ranks of older voters. For instance, Lester Thurow, noted M.I.T. economist, gloomily prophesized, "In the years ahead, class warfare is apt to be redefined as the young against the old, rather than the poor against the rich."

Former U.S. Secretary of Commerce and investment banker Peter Peterson is doing his best to provoke intergenerational conflict. Describing older persons as "invincible political titans," he envisions "retiring Boomers with inflated economic expectations and inadequate nest eggs, voting down school budgets, cannibalizing the nation's infrastructure and demanding ever-steeper hikes in payroll taxes." To combat "older titans," Peterson has used $1 billion of his personal fortune to establish a foundation that is attempting to organize a youthful political lobby to combat AARP and other old-age interest groups.

Robert H. Binstock, a political scientist, is professor of aging, health and society at Case Western Reserve University. A past president of the Gerontological Society of America and director of a White House Task Force on Older Americans, he is presently a member of the MacArthur Foundation's Research Network on an Aging Society. His latest book (co-authored with James H. Schulz) is *Aging Nation: The Economics and Politics of Growing Old in America*.

Up to now, numerous national surveys have shown strong multigenerational support for old-age benefit programs. Moreover, decades of voting data show no evidence of older persons voting as a cohesive, self-interested old-age benefits bloc. In fact, there has been evidence to the contrary, such as the 59 percent support President Reagan received from voters aged 65 and over in 1984 (contrasted with only 54 percent in 1980). This occurred even though Reagan had frozen the annual cost-of-living adjustment in Social Security benefits during his first term and proposed substantial future cuts in benefits.

However, the projected future costs of Social Security, and especially Medicare, could change all this. In the fiscal context of an extraordinarily high cumulative federal deficit, radical old-age policy reform proposals and legislation might very well emerge. This might include targeted tax increases and benefit cuts — such as rationing of coverage and care in Medicare — that could engender greater old-age group political cohesiveness and conflict between age groups. And this potential conflict could be exacerbated if the already substantial inequalities in income and access to healthcare in the United States keep increasing.

An inkling of how age-group political cohesiveness may develop could be observed during the protracted deliberations and debates over healthcare reform in 2009. From the outset of these discussions in the spring, President Obama frequently conveyed a message that the costs of reform would be mostly offset by savings in the Medicare program. This strong, overarching message from Obama was complemented in the summer by popular fears that government "death panels" would be established to decide whether to "pull the plug on granny" — fears planted and fanned by Republican opponents of reform. Various late-summer polls showed that many seniors had such concerns. And their fears were culturally ratified when the cover of *Newsweek* (9-21-09) was emblazoned with the headline "The Case for Killing Granny" and a photograph of a pulled plug. A fear of older-voter backlash may have influenced some freshman House Democrats to vote against healthcare reform because they expected to be especially vulnerable to Republican challenges when running for re-election without the benefit that they had from Obama's coattails in 2008.

The U.S. public needs to understand, for instance, what significant cutbacks in old-age policies could mean for the nature of family obligations and other familiar social institutions that are integral to the daily life of citizens of all ages.

Ultimately, of course, our future old-age policies will be shaped by the answers to two questions. First, will there be enough national wealth available to redistribute to older people? Second, will there be the political will to do so? That is, will the prevailing U.S. ideology support a politics of collectively insuring against the economic and health risks of old age? If we are to avoid intergenerational conflict, we need to strengthen that will.

A key strategy for strengthening the political will to support redistributive policies on aging is to undertake a broad educational initiative that helps the American people appreciate the extent to which our social contract — as expressed through so-called "old-age entitlements" — benefits all generations. Older people are not hermetically sealed from their families, communities and society. Neither are old-age benefits hermetically sealed from other age groups. The U.S. public needs to understand, for instance, what significant cutbacks in old-age policies could mean for the nature of family obligations and other familiar social institutions that are integral to the daily life of citizens of all ages.

What are some possible effects of major cuts in old-age benefit programs? Far more elderly persons than today would be financially dependent on their families and local institutions. Because of family financial necessities, we might see the return of three- and four-generation households, instead of preferred independent living arrangements. (In the context of our contemporary "Great Recession" we have already seen an increase in older persons moving in with their adult children, and vice versa.) Many adult children could be financially devastated by policy changes in federal and state old-age health insurance (including Medicaid as well as Medicare) that lead them to pay expensive costs of healthcare and long-term care for their parents. And such responsibilities for health expenses could, in turn, limit the resources available to adult children for raising their own children.

Social Security and old-age health insurance programs are not "luxurious" government benefits for a group of Americans that are often depicted in public rhetoric as if they were a separate, selfish tribe of "greedy geezers." At the same time, the evidence is clear that older people are among the taxpaying adult generations that support programs for our youth — such as children's health insurance, public education and many others. Effective dissemination of these broader, realistic contexts for perceiving government programs could go a long way toward moderating potential intergenerational conflict, and providing the political will to sustain essential multigenerational benefits in our aging society. ▣

POLITICS OF AGING REBORN: INSECURITY AND ANXIETY

————— Fernando Torres-Gil —————

n September 2009, *Newsweek* magazine's front cover displayed the headline "The Case for Killing Granny: Curbing Excessive End-of-Life Care is Good for America." This admittedly alarmist and sensationalized headline was meant to bring attention to the healthcare reform debates of that time and the spurious charges by Republicans that a proposed House bill would endorse "death panels." *Newsweek*'s inside story was analytical, substantive and well-balanced. It pointed out that the real issue is the need for all persons, regardless of age, to prepare for a longevity that would include end-of-life planning (e.g., advanced directives, living wills, trusts). Nonetheless, this headline brings back to the forefront the growing tensions of the pending old age of our next generation of elders: Boomers.

Much is said and written about this Boomer cohort, born between 1946 and 1964, a generation that will live longer than any previous cohort and will give us the greatest number of senior citizens (80 million), assuming we continue to use current definitions of being old (e.g., 65 years of age) (Gassoumis, et., al., 2010).[1]

Fernando Torres-Gil is associate dean of academic affairs at the School of Public Affairs, University of California, Los Angeles. He holds appointments as professor of social welfare and public policy in the School and is the director of the Center for Policy Research on Aging. Prior to joining UCLA, he was a professor of gerontology and public administration at the University of Southern California, where he continues as an adjunct professor of gerontology. He is the author of six books, including *The New Aging: Politics and Change in America* and *Lessons from Three Nations, Volumes I* and *II*.

There arise many fascinating issues and questions about the implications of this cohort's pending old age, but one that may well play out in the body politics will be their future interest and involvement in the political process. What does it mean that the electorate will, by 2029, have about 80 million voters over 65 years of age? Will they, can they, should they constitute an old-age bloc of voters focused on their old-age needs? Will we see a heightened level of advocacy predicated on old age? In short, will we see a revival of the politics of aging as we saw in the last century?

There are those who would argue *no*: 80 million individuals in this generation will have diffuse and disparate interests. Moreover, up to this point, members of this cohort have demonstrated little, if any, interest in the common concerns of their age group. Robert Binstock, the preeminent political scientist in gerontology, has consistently demonstrated that age does not correlate with political preferences. Yet, he and others do acknowledge that there may be situations around which today's elders coalesce around common concerns — generally the status of their Social Security and Medicare benefits (Schultz and Binstock 2006).[2]

It is in this regard that the healthcare reform debates of 2009 began to show the possibility of a politically charged old-age agenda. In the various Senate and House bills, a primary source of financing for expanding healthcare coverage was for those under 65 years

> **There arise many fascinating issues and questions about the implications of this cohort's pending old age, but one that may well play out in the body politics will be their future interest and involvement in the political process.**

of age to pay for it by reducing the growth of expenditures in the Medicare program and eliminating the subsidies in the Medicare Advantage program (which provide extra reimbursements to private, for-profit insurance companies to administer Medicare coverage to older persons). These proposals engendered opposition and deep concern by Medicare beneficiaries who felt they might see their benefits erode while those under 65 years of age would enjoy expanded healthcare coverage. Notwithstanding the endorsements by politically influential old-age lobby groups for healthcare reform — namely AARP and the National Committee to Preserve Medicare and Social Security — there remains a growing unease by persons over 65 years of age toward proposals to alter Medicare benefits and financing and, in time, toward reviewing the sustainability of the Social Security system.

This unease reflected, in part, a political reality facing the incumbent presidential administration. President Barack Obama, in his historic victory, was able to win over every age group except one: Voters 65 years of age and older favored the Republican John McCain over Obama, 51 percent to 47 percent. This contrasted with younger voters: Those ages 18 to 29 gave McCain 32 percent, and those ages 30 to 44 gave McCain 46 percent (New York Times, 2008).[3] This continues to be the case: Older voters remain more skeptical and less enamored of Obama's progressive agenda than do younger groups. In fact, one analyst predicts that the 2010 mid-term elections may heavily favor Republicans, "given that the electorate tends to be whiter and older than presidential elections" (Brownstein, 2009).[4]

What might such political data mean for the future politics of aging? Might we be seeing the beginnings of senior citizen activism predicated on common concerns? Should we have cause to worry about a future electorate that comprises upwards of 80 million voters? In fact, we may see an emerging political reawakening by today's middle-aged and young-old persons — though having more to do with insecurity and anxiety about their future old-age than about narrow self-interests centered on age.

We are on the cusp of an unprecedented retirement drama. Today's Boomers are not yet 65 years of age (this milestone begins in 2011), and they may well differ politically from today's older cohort, their parents and grandparents.

Much is written about their life passages, from new-found freedoms of expression and lifestyles to social and political activism and the defining moments of their formative years, including the civil rights movement, women's liberation, the Vietnam War and Watergate.

Clearly, not all Boomers were student activists or anti-war protestors. In fact, most led relatively normal lives as children, teenagers, young adults and middle-aged persons. But as a group, they did grow up in a time of relative prosperity and peace, and were spared the trauma and adversity faced by their parents during the Great Depression, World War II and the Cold War (Dychtwald, K and J. Flower, 1989; Kotlikoff, L.K. and S. Burns, 2004; Hudson, 2005; Light, 1988).[5] And in reality, this cohort has benefited from the legacy of that "Greatest Generation": one which saved the nation from external and internal threats, invested in the great social and physical infrastructures that made America prosperous (e.g., highways, public schools, the GI Bill) and allowed their offspring to live their lives off this legacy. That "Greatest Generation" is retired and passing away, yet its legacy also included the politics of aging that gave rise to a senior citizen movement that, in turn, gave us public benefits that dramatically lowered poverty rates among the elderly and insured a modicum of personal security in retirement. Such benefits include

Social Security, Medicare, Medicaid, the Older Americans Act, unemployment compensation, Supplemental Security Income and defined benefit retirement plans.

The major issue facing the pending aging of Boomers will be quite stark: Will Boomers have a social safety net in their old age commensurate with that of their parents and grandparents? Will this next generation of elders have a retirement equal to, or better than, that of their parents? The potential answers are not rosy. We are facing the real possibility that Boomers may grow old with less security and comfort than their elders.

A fraying social safety net; unsustainable fiscal pressures on Social Security and Medicare; the demise of defined benefit plans for pensions and retiree healthcare; the volatile nature of defined contribution plans (e.g., 401ks); the dramatic decline of real estate values and home equity; and the need to keep working longer than planned all portend the possibility of a new level of anxiety and insecurity among the next generation of older persons. Add to that the unprecedented annual federal deficits and accumulating national debt, and the decline in the nation's global prestige and power. Now we have the real possibility that the country may not be able to afford expanding old-age benefits for twice as many older persons as we now have, much less afford what we now have.

Another ingredient to this mix will be the emergence of diversity as a hallmark of the nation with a mostly minority population of young workers supporting older, mostly non-minority retirees (Treas and Torres-Gil, 2009).[6] In short, we may see an ironic twist of fate: While today's elders faced their great test of adversity in their youth (the 1930s to the 1950s), Boomers may face their great generational test of adversity in their old age (from 2010 to 2030 and beyond).

How they meet this test will define the political landscape of the next several decades.

Taken together, we may have the seeds of a new politics of aging. Boomers, as they become old, may begin to find common cause around their frustrations and disillusionments about living longer, but growing older and less secure than their parents. Should this admittedly negative scenario occur, then we are faced with some important political questions: How might upward of 80 million old-age voters respond to these challenges? Will they be susceptible to demagogic appeals by self-interested promoters with narrow agendas? Will the next generation of elders use their votes to force public demands on the U.S. Congress that expand their benefits and taxes on the shoulders of a younger and more diverse population? Or might this generation of older voters find common cause around intergenerational, interethnic and interracial coalitions promoting a broader social agenda for all persons in need?

The answers to these questions may well define the political future of the United States in the next 10 to 30 years. Hopefully, the troubling generational tensions evident in the debates around healthcare reform in 2009-2010 will not be precursors to a politics of aging that is selfish and narcissistic, but rather one that will be inclusive and focused on what is best for the nation. Only time will tell, but what is likely to occur is a revival of a politics of aging that will be based on the needs and expectations of a new generation of older persons. 🖎

Endnotes
1.   Gassoumos, Z. Wilbur, K., and Torres-Gil, F. (2010). "Who are the Latino Baby Boomers? Demographic and Economic Characteristics of a Hidden Population". *Journal of Aging Social Policy 22* (1) Forthcoming.
2.   Shultz, J. and R Binstock (2006). *Aging Nation: The Economics and Politics of Growing Older in America.* Praeger: Westport, CT.
3.   *New York Times* (2008). Election Results, 2008.

4. Brownstein, R. "The Gray Cloud". *National Journal* October 3, 2009, pp. 76.
5. Dychtwald, K and J. Flower. *Age Wave: The Challenges and Opportunities of an Aging America*. Jeremy P. Tarcher, Inc. Los Angeles, CA .1989. / Kotlfokoff, L.. and S. Burns. *The Coming Generational Storm: What You Need to Know about America's Economic Future*. The MIT Press, Cambridge, MA. 2004. / Hudson, R. (Ed.) *The New Politics of Old Age Policy*. The John Hopkins University Press: Baltimore, MD. 2005. / Moody, H.R. *Aging: Concepts and Controversies*. (5th Edition) Forge Press, Thousand Oaks, CA. 2006. / Light, P.C. *Baby Boomers*. W.W. Norton and Co., Inc. New York, NY. 1988.
6. Treas, J., and F. Torres-Gil (2009). Immigration in an Aging Society. *Generations*. Vol. 32, No 4.

Bibliography

- Brownstein, R. "The Gray Cloud". *National Journal*. October 3, 2009, pp. 76.
- Dychtwald, K. and J. Flower. *Age Wave: The Challenges and Opportunities of an Aging America*. Jeremy P. Tarcher, Inc. Los Angeles, CA, 1989.
- Gassoumos, Z. Wilbur, K., and Torres-Gil, F. "Who are the Latino Baby Boomers? Demographic and Economic Characteristics of a Hidden Population". *Journal of Aging Social Policy*. 22 (1) Forthcoming, 2010.
- Hudson, R.B. (ed.). *The New Politics of Old Age Policy*. Baltimore: Johns Hopkins University Press, 2005.
- Kotlifokoff, L.J. and S. Burns. *The Coming Generational Storm: What You Need to Know about America's Economic Future*. The MIT Press, Cambridge, MA, 2004.
- Light, P.C. *Baby Boomers*. W.W. Norton and Co., Inc. New York, NY, 1988.
- Moody, H.R. *Aging: Concepts and Controversies*. (5th Edition) Forge Press, Thousand Oaks, CA, 2006.
- Treas, J. and F. Torres-Gil (eds.). "Immigration in an Aging Society". *Generations* Vol. 32, No 4. 2009.

MEDICARE'S NOT-SO-HIDDEN VIRUS: HEALTHCARE COSTS

—————— Daniel Callahan ——————

W e have known for decades that it is coming. The Baby Boom Generation will, by the millions, soon become Medicare beneficiaries. The trustees of the program have pleaded for years that its future solvency requires an immediate effort to control its ever-rising costs; start sooner, not later. The newly elected President Obama put the issue of cost control at the top of his healthcare reform agenda, both parties early on recognized its importance, and public opinion polls underlined its urgency. The former secretary of U.S. Health and Human Services, Michael O. Leavitt, said in November 2008 that Medicare is "heading for disaster," and a number of policy analysts have said in recent years that nothing less than a doubling of taxes or a radical cut in benefits can save Medicare in the long run.

Forewarned is forearmed, it is said. Not so in this case. As the various reform proposals focused on cost control in general and Medicare in particular made their way into the House and Senate bills they declined in number and potency. Access and overall reform costs came to dominate the debate. When cost issues arose, it soon became clear that Congress had little taste for taking on the assorted

Daniel Callahan is research scholar and president emeritus of The Hastings Center, which he cofounded, and elected member of the National Academy of Sciences. He is the author of many books, including *Medicine and the Market* and most recently *Taming the Beloved Beast: How Medical Technology Costs Are Destroying Our Health Care System*.

business, professional and public interest groups that sought to undermine tough proposals. When push came to shove they shared a common agenda: resist any and all but the most inoffensive and innocuous methods of cost control.

Prevention and information technology met that low standard. Doctors are not to have cuts in Medicare reimbursements, not much will be taken from hospitals, and President Obama went out of his way — with uncommon bipartisan support — to assure Medicare recipients there will be no cuts in their benefits.

Put bluntly, the necessary hard work of controlling Medicare costs has barely begun, and it has probably been made all the harder by legislators who have worked overtime to assure the elderly that all is well, that nothing will be taken from them. Hardly anything is more fearful for members of Congress — the congressional debate made clear — than alienating the elderly, obviously a large, vocal and growing constituency. Far from taking even one tiny step toward increasing taxes or cutting benefits, it is likely to be harder than ever to take steps of any kind.

Where does that leave us? As a practical matter, as the financial woes of Medicare increase, Congress may be forced into some incremental tactics: to enact small ad hoc "emergency" tax increases to stave off its projected insolvency in eight years; to continue raising copayments and deductibles; to pick on hospitals; and to nibble

> **Put bluntly, the necessary hard work of controlling Medicare costs has barely begun, and it has probably been made all the harder by legislators who have worked overtime to assure the elderly that all is well, that nothing will be taken from them.**

away at physician reimbursement, training programs and nursing care. The aim will be to walk a fine line between the incitement of muttering and that of outright loud indignation of a kind to be remembered at election time.

Leadership will be hard to come by. No legislator is likely to court a reputation as a tough cost cutter, particularly of patient benefits. Even now, many of the Medicare cuts in reform legislation have a delayed starting date and are meant to have an impact only over at least a decade. In the meantime, of course the baseline of costs will continue to rise and will, at the end of that decade, be much higher than at present even if the rate of future cost increases has been slowed.

There are at present two major obstacles to going much further than that. One of them is the powerful resistance to using the array of methods that European countries employ to contain costs. They include price controls on drugs; negotiated physician fees; careful management of the introduction and deployment of new technologies; national budgets; and hospital spending limits — and not incidentally a lesser fixation than is our wont on new technologies and on media attention to health issues. All of that is buttressed by a public far less hostile to government than are many Americans. Unless our attitude changes, the tested measures of controlling cost, which are widely used elsewhere, will not be available here.

The other obstacle is even more daunting, and is beginning to affect even those European countries able to deploy the most effective means of cost control. It is the triple threat of the imminent retirement of the Baby Boom Generation; the never-ending development and diffusion of new technologies to keep them alive; and the high expectations — and with it a high sense of entitlement — that medical progress must of necessity bring them better health. The number of

Medicare beneficiaries is projected to rise from 46 million to 79 million over the next 20 years, and their costs from $502 billion to $937 billion. Cancer, stroke and heart disease treatments are now expensively and almost routinely saving the lives of those in their 80s and 90s — but usually not curing their disease, only allowing them a longer survival time with continuing expensive medical care.

Medical progress, hailed for years as the answer to rising costs, turns out to be its main driver. And in case one thinks the future will see a corner turned, the Congressional Budget Office in a 2008 study said that "examples of new treatments for which long-term savings have been clearly demonstrated are few ... improvements in medical care that decrease mortality ... paradoxically increase overall spending on health care because surviving patients live longer and therefore use health services for more years."

The war against death can not be won, and now its main entranceway, old age, cannot be made as debris-free as we might like.

"Abandon hope, all ye who enter here?" Well, it just looks that way because at the moment it is. The hopeful talk of ridding our system of waste and inefficiency; getting rid of fee-for-service medicine; bundling and integrating the treatment of chronic illness; and developing cost-conscious medical consumers have much to say for it — but not enough by far to defuse the Baby-Boom time bomb.

The trouble is that we have become infatuated with progress-driven, innovation-infatuated medicine, cultivated for well over a century now, that is turning out to be unaffordable. The war against death can not be won, and now its main entranceway, old age, cannot be made as debris-free as we might like. Nothing less than a more moderate, finite vision of medical possibilities is necessary:

one that does not entail ever-rising costs or onerously increased tax burdens on the young to support the old; and that does end utopian fantasies about a transformation of old age. Recognition of the coming necessity of Medicare rationing would be a first step in that direction. It would be wonderful if further steps could be achieved without going through the disaster that former HHS Secretary Leavitt sees coming. My guess is that it might take nothing less to bring us to our senses about managing Medicare costs. ◉

THE GREAT RETIREMENT DIVIDE

—————— Richard Adler ——————

During the next decade or so, millions of Boomers will reach their mid-60s, the traditional age of retirement. What will they do? According to multiple surveys, a large majority of Boomers — by some reports as many as 70 or 80 percent — say that they don't want to retire at 65, but intend to continue working to age 70 or beyond. Many say that "they never want to retire."

But what will actually happen with Boomers and retirement? Will they stay in their current jobs — if they can — or shift to new jobs, or quit working altogether? The answer to this question has big implications for our economy, for employers and, of course, for Boomers themselves. As I've watched my own friends and acquaintances reach their mid-60s and deal with the question of retiring, I'm seeing a pattern that suggests what may happen on a larger scale.

First, almost everyone who has had a job that provided them with decent, secure pensions and other benefits has tended to take a traditional retirement. This category includes public sector employees (teachers, military personnel, government workers) along with a steadily decreasing number of people who have had entire careers with a single, large company that offered good benefits. Their pensions, along with Social Security and their own savings, have been

Richard Adler is principal of People & Technology, a research and consulting firm in Silicon Valley. He is also a research affiliate at the Institute for the Future in Palo Alto, California, where he co-leads a project on "Baby Boomers: The Next 20 Years."

sufficient to allow them to retire in relative comfort. In addition, their employers often have policies that actively encourage employees to opt for retirement at a certain age.

A second, smaller group consists of people who, either as a result of hard work or good luck (or, often, a combination of both) have struck it rich, or at least rich enough to not need to work to maintain themselves and their families.

Some individuals in these two fortunate groups have chosen to pursue personal interests like travel or a hobby or spending more time with family after retirement. (One admirable friend, after a successful career in high tech, went back to school to earn a doctoral degree in English literature in order to pursue his passion for 18th century poetry.) Others have explored new work opportunities. But in all cases, people in these categories have had the luxury to choose what they want to do with their later years, which may or may not involve working for money.

Then there is everyone else. In this much larger group are those of us who have worked for multiple employers or for employers who have not offered a package of "defined benefits" that included a guaranteed pension; or who have worked for themselves for all or a good part of their lives. People in this group are largely dependent on their savings if they want to stop working. We know that Boomers as a group have been notoriously poor savers, and only a fraction have been able to accumulate enough resources to finance a secure retirement. And the recent recession has dealt a severe blow even to those who believed that they had saved enough to provide them with financial independence. (A blogger for the Canadian *Financial Post*, who has published "The Wealthy Boomer" for more than 10 years, recently suggested, not entirely facetiously, that he was changing the name of his blog to "The Formerly Wealthy Boomer.")

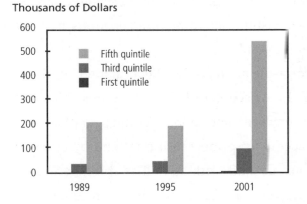

MEDIAN NET WORTH OF BOOMER HOUSEHOLDS

Thousands of Dollars

Fifth quintile
Third quintile
First quintile

Source: AARP, "The Distribution of Financial Wealth Among Boomers," 2004

For many, if not most Boomers, traditional retirement is becoming a relatively meaningless concept. Working past the age of 65 is becoming more of an expectation than an exception. What form work in later life will take remains an unanswered question. Some may wish to keep working just as they have been for as long as possible. But age matters, both physically and psychologically, and it is common for people as they move through their 60s to shift their priorities in terms of the kind of work they want to do and how much time they spend doing it. After decades of "earning a living" it is not uncommon for people to become more interested in the significance of their work and in achieving a better work/life balance. Some have become interested in finding "good work" — jobs in the nonprofit sector that generate income *and* have high social value. Others have chosen to keep working in the same field, but on a part-time basis.

Unfortunately, there remains a paucity of resources to help people keep working in later life in ways that are satisfying to them and economically productive. It is noteworthy that high school seniors are able to get help from college counselors in finding places to go after they graduate, and college seniors have access to placement offices that help them find work after they graduate. But, as of yet, there are few institutions to help older adults navigate the terrain beyond "retirement."

One promising model is the "Next Chapter" initiative, sponsored by the San Francisco-based Civic Ventures. This initiative helps older adults explore their options for the next phase of their lives by providing access to support resources and by connecting them to opportunities for paid work as well as volunteering. Several dozen prototype projects have been launched in recent years. (A directory of Next Chapter projects in 10 states around the country is online at www.civicventures.org.)

Another useful resource for older workers is an online course, developed jointly by AARP's Kentucky state office and "ed2go," a provider of online educational programs. "Making Age an Asset in Your Job Search" (www.ed2go.com/workafter50) helps older workers understand the challenges they face, gives an overview of the current job market, and provides practical guidance with tasks like creating an effective resume and preparing for a job interview.

And one of my favorite examples of a "new way to work" is "YourEncore," a company set up by alumni of Procter & Gamble and Eli Lilly that recruits technical professionals who have retired from full-time employment and markets them to companies as consultants to address specific problems. Companies that use the services of YourEncore gain access to highly talented experts on a short-term, focused basis, while the participants get to work on interesting projects and earn money, but on their own schedules. The motto of YourEncore is "People don't retire anymore; they just go on to do other things."

It is unlikely the old model of retirement will disappear entirely. The ever-shrinking number of those who have the means to do so may well choose to follow the traditional path. But this model will be neither appealing nor practical for the great majority of those who move into their 60s and beyond in the next several decades. New resources and new policies will be needed to accommodate them. The initiatives described here are just small steps that respond to the massive need among aging Boomers to remain productive past the traditional age of retirement — both for their own sake and the sake of our society.

But more change is coming. As Sarah Harper with the Oxford University Institute on Aging has said, "By 2030 we will look back and realize that the end of the 20th century [when] people were retiring at 60 was a blip — people will simply have to work longer. There is nothing to suggest that at the age of 70 you perform tasks less well than at 20. The idea of falling off the perch at 65 is rubbish. ▣

OUR WORKFORCE IS AGING; GROW WITH IT

—— David Baxter ——

How can we create the necessary foundation for sustained economic growth and financial security as we emerge from our current recession? Just as new capital realities have required a restructuring of the capital markets, new demographic realities will require a radical rethinking of both the value and role of older workers and even of retirement itself.

The current economic reckoning comes upon us at a unique moment in time. The Boomer Generation — the largest generation in history — now stands at the threshold of traditional retirement. What happens when 77 million Boomers begin to retire? Can our nation afford to support millions of new retirees? What happens to our productivity and innovation as some of the most skilled, knowledgeable and hardworking employees permanently disappear from the workforce?

Earlier this year, Age Wave, a research and consulting firm specializing in population aging and the age 50-plus marketplace, conducted a research study canvassing more than 2,000 Americans. The goal was to better understand the impact of the recent economic

David Baxter is a senior vice president at Age Wave, a research and consulting firm specializing in population aging and the age 50-plus marketplace. He has developed and managed numerous highly acclaimed national and global surveys, uncovering trends and unique market opportunities created by the growth of the over-50 population. He also is coauthor of the *Handbook of the New American Workforce*, as well as a public speaker on cutting-edge research findings.

crisis on their lives. We found that today's pre-retirees believe that they will now need to postpone their retirement 4.2 years on average, which would be the first time in history that retirement age significantly increased in America. And, 70 percent reported that they *wanted* to continue working in some form during their retirement. Americans are clearly beginning to re-vision both the timing and purpose of retirement. But are policymakers, organizations and corporate leaders waking up to these new realities?

In the 1970s, Boomers began to enter the workforce in significant numbers, replacing the much smaller cohort — born during the Great Depression and World War II — that preceded them. The impact was both immense and pervasive; the pool of available workers increased by 29 percent in a single decade. Workforce growth remained strong in the remaining decades of the 20th century as the influx of younger Boomers continued to buttress the numbers of workers.

Today, however, workforce growth is coming to a virtual standstill. From an increase of 29 percent in the 1970s, America's workforce will grow only 12 percent in the current decade and will increase a mere 4 percent in the next decade. The collapse in workforce growth is the simple result of demographics. In the current decade, the population of adults age 18-34 will increase by just 7 percent. In the next decade (2010-2020), the age 18-34 population will grow a mere 3 percent. The era of an

> We found that today's pre-retirees believe that they will now need to postpone their retirement 4.2 years on average, which would be the first time in history that retirement age significantly increased in America.

unending supply of young workers is clearly over. We will need older workers to remain productive as a country.

Moreover, as the Boomer Generation enters into their retirement years in greater and greater numbers, companies of all sizes will confront a massive "brain drain" of skills, know-how among their most experienced workers, and experienced management. Nearly seven million talented people in key managerial, professional and technical jobs may exit the workforce in the next 10 years.

Where will we find our workers in the years ahead? The only population that will demonstrate substantial growth in the next decade is those age 55- plus.

Where will we find our workers in the years ahead? The only population that will demonstrate substantial growth in the next decade is those age 55-plus. Fueled by the aging of the Baby Boom Generation, the number of adults age 55 and older will increase 27 percent between 2010 and 2020.

Yet, despite the increasing shortage of young workers and unprecedented growth of available mature workers, organizations continue to focus their recruiting and development efforts on the younger workforce. According to a survey by Manpower Inc., only 18 percent of employers in the United States have strategies in place to recruit older workers, and less than a third has implemented any retention strategies for their older workforce.

Some innovative thought-leaders and cutting-edge organizations are beginning to recognize the need to shift their workforce policies to fit the new demographic realities. Companies are increasingly realizing the value of mature workers. In the "Future of Retirement Study," a global survey completed in 2006 on retirement and work, employers said that mature workers were just as productive and motivated as younger workers, and were even more loyal and reliable. Some leading-edge companies and organizations are beginning to develop best practices for recruiting, engaging, motivating and retaining mature workers.

Age Wave identified five key best practices for creating a workforce and organization to compete in the next decade.

First, organizations must become expert at forecasting key workforce aging and retirement trends and the potential risks to their business. According to the Society for Human Resource Management, less than a third of human resources professionals have charted their organization's demographic makeup. Companies that do not conduct this analysis can be blindsided by the rapid workforce aging and related talent shortages projected for the next decade.

Second, organizations must improve their capability to recruit mature workers. Review *promotional* language for jobs with implicit or explicit references to employee age. Older workers are more likely to be attracted to advertisements emphasizing "experience," "knowledge" and "expertise" and to interpret those stressing "energy," "willingness to learn" and "high ambition" as implicitly targeting younger workers. Also, assess job promotion channels. Recruiting older workers sometimes requires operating through nontraditional channels or creative partnerships with professional societies or other groups with memberships that skew older.

Third, implement flex-retirement programs to attract, retain and motivate older workers. Organizations often can convince valued older workers to delay retirement by offering them "flex-retirement options" that provide greater work style flexibility and more control over their time. Examples include reduced hours or schedules, temporary work, consulting assignments, job sharing, telecommuting, mentoring positions and other special positions and assignments that would be attractive to key mature employees. These programs can help retain key valuable employees, provide access to industry knowledge and expertise through mentoring programs, and tap into highly experienced temporary talent pools of retirees.

Fourth, design benefits strategies that are compatible with flex-retirement programs. In August 2006, the U.S. Congress passed the Pension Protection Act. Prior to this act, employees were unable to receive distributions from defined pension plans before the pension plan's normal retirement age if they continued to work for the organization. Under the new law, employees age 62 and older may receive defined benefit plans while continuing to work, making the implementation of flex-retirement programs far less cumbersome. After passage of this law, nearly half of employers re-evaluated their flex-retirement options, according to a survey by Hewitt Associates, Inc. Although the Pension Protection Act facilitates the creation of flex retirement programs, there remain key issues employers need to carefully consider. For example, health benefits can be strong incentives to keep an employee working; even if covered by Medicare, many older workers will work to continue to receive health coverage for dependents.

And finally, organizations must build management practices and a culture to motivate an older workforce. Build a culture that values experience. Companies that have been the most successful in creating programs that leverage the skills of their older workers have a deep corporate culture that values older worker capabilities. Include aging and generational issues as components of managerial and diversity training, and review human resources policies to make sure they do not discriminate against older workers. Examine promotion policies, salary calculations, performance review procedures and benefits to ensure they are not implicitly or explicitly biased against older employees. Develop a culture of continuous career development. Mature employees are more likely to stay loyal and motivated if they feel they have room for advancement. And offer continued learning and training opportunities. Mature workers often are overlooked for training and education because managers feel employees nearing retirement age are not worth the investment of additional training resources. A recent U.S. Bureau of Labor Statistics study found that workers 55 years and older receive half as much training as younger workers — yet turnover among older workers is actually lower than that among younger workers.

The next decade will be a time of unprecedented challenge and opportunity for both policymakers and corporate leaders as we begin to confront new workforce realities. As our economy begins to normalize, organizations that continue to ignore demographic changes in the workforce and maintain strategies and policies optimized for a younger workforce will increasingly experience critical talent shortages and retention problems. Conversely, organizations that reshape their recruitment, engagement, work structures and cultures to attract and retain the new mature workforce will be well positioned to capitalize on unprecedented growth opportunities in a vast pool of experienced and valuable workers.

WILL GENERATIONAL COVERAGE
SURVIVE THE MEDIA MELTDOWN?

i———— Paul Kleyman ————i

"**M**y prediction is that five years from now the fact that America is aging won't be news anymore. It will be a fact, like the sun rising every morning," asserts one veteran journalist who covers generational issues.

"I would say there is less coverage of aging because newspapers are folding left and right," says another of equal prominence. And a third reply to my email query about the state of what journalists call the "generations" or "age beat," says this, "To be honest, I don't feel as if anyone knows what's going to happen in media next year, much less five years from now. We will all be surprised. We still need to fight the good fight, though."

Who among my highly knowledgeable informants has it right? Like the classic Akira Kurosawa film, "Rashomon," in which each character sees the same crime from a unique perspective, none of the above journalists is wrong. I have tracked the coverage of aging and ageism in the news and information media for more than two decades. During this time I've seen signs of improvement in the uphill swim against the current of anti-aging *crème* that permeates American culture. In 1993, I was among a small number of journalists,

---

Paul Kleyman directs the Ethnic Elders Newsbeat at New America Media, the news service for 3,000 U.S. ethnic media. Previously, he edited *Aging Today*, newspaper of the American Society on Aging, for 20 years. He co-founded and is national coordinator of the Journalists Network on Generations and edits its e-newsletter, *Generations Beat Online*.

passionate about the undiscovered subject of aging, who formed a group now called the "Journalists Network on Generations." Many of us were in midlife. My surveys as late as 2002 showed the average reporter on the age beat had been a professional journalists for 22 years, and quite a few had personally experienced generational or caregiving issues.

Journalists who covered generational concerns overall believed that the aging of the huge Boomer Generation (and potential advertising market) would eventually crack through the gray ceiling of the youth-obsessed media that artificially held down the coverage.

What few anticipated, though, was the financial collapse of the media, an effect of calcified and unresponsive old forms being chiseled to bits and bytes by new media formats. Free and instantaneous Internet access can bring anyone an astonishing array of information, including original research and analysis previously available only to experts, not to mention easy links to dozens of articles from far flung news sources every day.

To understand why the massive longevity revolution — the addition of three decades to average life expectancy within a single century — has received relatively scant attention in news columns, it is important to, in the phrase of Watergate journalists, Woodward and Bernstein, "follow the money." Institutional biases are always at least partly perpetuated by rationalized financial mechanisms. That is, conventions justifying business practices that are either long outmoded or, perhaps, were ill-founded in the first place.

Stark examples are the 20th century practice of red-lining in real estate to keep Jews or African Americans from "bringing down property values" in white neighborhoods, or the "planned obsolescence" that eventually drove Detroit automakers into the ground against competition from more durable imports from Europe and Japan. And how about the folly of Wall Street's "self-correcting" market economy? In media, market hubris manifests in the myth of youth as a perpetual revenue machine — the vaunted 18-to-49 age group, especially audiences 18-34. New media and the aging of the Boomer Generation, with its high levels of disposable income, are cracking through concrete market conventions like green new life.

What most people who have heard of the seasonal "sweeps weeks" and "ratings wars" don't know is that the advertising industry applies demographic findings — showing so many viewers by gender, ethnicity and especially age — in a way that devalues every 1,000 estimated sets of eyeballs as they get older. Many remember that in 2002, ABC-TV failed to lure David Letterman away from CBS. What was page-one entertainment news for days obscured the fact that the ABC program Letterman would have replaced, "Nightline" with Ted Koppel, actually had a 10 percent larger audience than "The Late Show" with David Letterman. The catch: Because of the age-skewed TV ratings, the same 30-second spot that drew $30,000 on "Nightline" would pull $40,000 for Letterman's somewhat younger audience.

What's age got to do with entertainment and news? Few leading roles in entertainment or participants in reality TV have matured beyond young adulthood. For example, over the years, broadcast reporters for both national and local news told me that their requests to do more stories on aging were turned down because attracting additional older viewers would diminish ad revenues.

In the late 1990s I learned from a former reporter at *U.S. News & World Report* that an editor there had invoked a "no prune-face rule." Reporters for that editor's section were told not to bring in stories with photos including too many people who looked to be over 50. That was then, but last fall a reporter at another mainstream news organization told me that an editorial executive there admonishes staff to avoid getting too many "gray hairs" into stories.

The misconception of two elderly people on their rockers, who can't offer much to new markets does not match today's midlife and older Boomers' real spending on travel, home businesses, health products, continuing education and many another areas — especially on their grandchildren. Sure, there are age-specific ads for retirement planning or prescription drugs, but generally the ad industry largely discounts older adults as part of the social landscape.

As for content in TV and film, the sea is beginning to change, albeit slowly. By early 2010, aging Boomers were turning up in television programs such as "Men of a Certain Age" and "Saving Grace" and in big screen hits, such as "It's Complicated" with Meryl Streep and Alec Baldwin.

If late-night lucre from talk-show ad dollars proves a rough barometer of change, a key structural alteration in network advertising seems to have emerged along the Leno-Letterman axis. NBC's installation of Jay Leno at 10 p.m. nightly in 2009, with the younger Conan O'Brien flailing his comic elbows as if against Letterman, faltered badly. Even though O'Brien did capture more of the desired 18-34 male audience, the stiff competition for young men from video games, cable, the Internet and other new

The misconception of two elderly people on their rockers, who can't offer much to new markets does not match today's midlife and older Boomers' real spending on travel, home businesses, health products, continuing education and many another areas — especially on their grandchildren.

media has shrunk the average network TV audience across the board. *The New York Times* reported that Leno's lackluster ratings at 10 p.m., and the defection of many older viewers from O'Brien to Letterman, meant that the coveted young-adult audience was being newly regarded not as advertising gold but merely as a niché market. At least some of the financial pressures to wake up and smell the Boomer demographics have come from the prime NBC audience: its affiliate stations. Local stations were losing advertising dollars because of NBC's poorer than promised carry-over ratings from Leno's new show to local newscasts.

This is only one manifestation of the complicated business arrangements that can affect who sees what faces or coverage in the media. There is no guarantee that the eventual benefits from the explosion of new media will accrue to older audiences. But signs are that the underpinnings of stilted media economic models are finally rotting away.

The media movement toward the affluent Boomer market is also inching up the columns of mainstream news media, after more that two decades of fruitless youth chasing. As recently as 2005, Northwestern University's Readership Institute, which conducts the largest ongoing study of newspaper readership (financed by the Newspaper Association of America and other media organizations) urged publishers to attract younger readers by redesigning their publications as "experience papers," that is, relating articles more directly to the lifestyles of desired audiences. The managing director of the institute noted that newspapers were serving older, more loyal readers "at the expense of younger, less frequent readers." That conclusion was at odds with actual practice: too little coverage of vital changes to meet the needs of an aging society.

Signs of progress are emerging. Award-winning journalist Maureen West, who left the *Arizona Republic* as one of its top editors in 2008 and now freelances for major national media, observes that Gannett newspapers, such as her former employer and *USA Today*, "are all targeted toward people 45 and older because they know they need those readers to support their print products if they are to have a future."

The future of newspapers is precarious, of course, with 140 having stopped the presses in 2009 and gone strictly online. Regarding the Internet, though, West notes her Google Alert set for "baby boomer women" yields 10 stories or more each day, and predicted "that we will increasingly find more stories about or of interest to people 50 and older, but they won't be identifiable as stories on the age beat. They will be part of every beat. It will be like the health care coverage today."

The future of newspapers is precarious, of course, with 140 having stopped the presses in 2009 and gone strictly online.

Sharing West's optimism, although more cautiously, is John Wasik, author of 13 books and former personal finance columnist for *Bloomberg News*. "I believe there will be greater focus on transitional issues — moving from retirement back into the workforce, full employment to part-time working, downsizing, and so on," he says, adding, "Without a doubt there will be even more specialized media sites devoted to these issues and perhaps Yahoo and Google will become original content providers."

However optimistic Wasik is for the long run, skepticism grounds his understanding of current developments in media. He observed, "No matter where you go — mainstream press, the trades, academia — it seems like there's this perverse groupthink to reward mediocrity and compliance." One news company he worked for hired a media consulting firm "to gin up some metrics as to how they should be performing. Editors were then compensated on the number of 'hits' their team was getting, measured by how much attention each story got on the system. That kills innovation and decent writing," Wasik warns, "and reduces editors to accountants."

Also less than enthused by media trends toward coverage of aging issues, Elizabeth Pope, a national freelance writer, relates: "About five years ago, I was selling stories on caregiving, housing, workplace issues, brain health, fitness, etc., to a whole range of markets or magazine sections that don't exist now or have been redesigned to appeal to a younger demographic." Pope noted for example, that *Time Magazine* and the *Los Angeles Times* discontinued their special sections on retirement, observing, "Advertisers want young eyeballs, and they don't care who's got all the money to buy luxury cars, cruises, fine jewelry and so on."

Boomer marketing experts predict that future discretionary spending will be controlled by older, healthier, more discerning consumers. In spite of that assessment, "Advertisers continue to seek youth markets," notes Maria D. Vesperi, an anthropology professor at New College of Florida and authority on aging/media issues. "This is an economically damaging trend for traditional news media, which face steadily aging audiences and decreased attention to news among post-Boomer generations."

Furthermore, says Cleveland-based freelancer Eileen Beal, "Age-beat coverage seems to be morphing into reporting on health and healthcare issues affecting the elderly." She continued, "My guess is that writers who are covering aging are going to find fewer outlets in real journalism — that is, newspapers — and more in markets with specialty publications aimed at seniors or retirees," including worthy but non-journalistic informational materials for government and nonprofit service agencies.

A more sanguine viewpoint is shared by independent video producer Bailey Barash, a former senior executive producer at CNN, who says, "I think age-beat coverage will gather increasing attention from all users of news because the numbers of age-beat consumers are rapidly increasing. Many of those 50 and above have learned by now that they have to be their own advocates and will support the coverage, creation and dissemination of information about their generation and its issues." Specifically, Barash sees greater support for Web-based media. "The 50-plus have worked with digital media and the Internet long enough now to be comfortable with a smorgasbord of information choices and to use them to make decisions that will help them keep jobs and savings, and make better healthcare, lifestyle and investment choices."

And what will be the incentive to pay journalists for news gathering and analysis on generational issues? Wasik allows, "I'm actually optimistic. I truly believe that those journalists who are multidisciplinary, compassionate, curious and willing to dig down a few layers are still going to do well. Health policy, finance, retirement, technology have not gotten any simpler and we still need some ace interpreters out there to tell us what's going on in plain language."

MEDICAL

IS GOOGLE MAKING US SMART OR STUPID?

Gary W. Small, M.D.

F or most of my professional career, I've been developing technologies to help us understand how the brain functions and changes as we age. Our UCLA research group has invented brain scanning techniques that can detect the earliest stages of Alzheimer's disease decades before people experience obvious symptoms (Bookheimer et al, 2000; Small et al, 2006). Our goal is to identify candidates for prevention treatments so we can protect a healthy brain — a strategy that I think will be more feasible than attempting to repair the aging brain once neurodegenerative damage sets in (Small et al, 2008).

In recent years, I also have been struck by how other new technologies have transformed our lives. Mobile phones and laptop computers — along with email, text and instant messaging, video games, social networking, and other dazzling programs — make our lives more efficient and entertaining. Yet we know very little about how these new technologies may be affecting our brains. We do know

Gary W. Small, M.D. is a professor of psychiatry at the UCLA Semel Institute and directs the Memory and Aging Research Center and the UCLA Center on Aging. He is the author and coauthor of numerous articles and books, including *The Memory Bible*, *The Memory Prescription*, *The Longevity Bible* and *iBrain*. *Scientific American* magazine named him one of the world's top innovators in science and technology. Dr. Small invented the first brain scan that allows doctors to see the physical evidence of brain aging and Alzheimer's disease in living people. Among his numerous breakthrough research studies, he now leads a team of neuroscientists who are demonstrating that exposure to computer technology causes rapid and profound changes in brain neural circuitry.

that the brain at any age is sensitive to sensory stimulation from moment to moment, so I have wondered about the effects of this constant tech exposure.

Such effects may be particularly profound for young brains, which are still being formed and creating their basic neural pathways. The average young person spends at least nine hours each day using some type of technology. And often the technology is so new that their parents don't use it nor do they understand it. We are witnessing the traditional generation gap transform into a "brain gap," which separates *digital natives*, young people born into a world of 24/7 technology, and *digital immigrants*, those of us who come to computers and digital technology as adults (Small & Vorgan, 2008).

To better understand these potential technology brain effects, our UCLA research group decided to study the brain's neural circuitry response to a common computer task—searching the Internet (Small et al, 2009; Moody et al, 2009). We recruited middle-aged volunteers with similar backgrounds. Half of them had experience searching the Internet, while the other half had no experience. As they underwent functional magnetic resonance imaging scans (MRIs), study participants performed both book-reading tasks and Web searches.

The MRIs revealed that all the volunteers showed similar brain activity during the book-reading task in regions controlling vision, memory and language, but Internet searches revealed a major difference between the two groups. The Web-savvy group registered much greater activity throughout the brain, especially in the frontal areas that control decision-making and complex reasoning compared with the other group that had no computer experience. In part two of this study, we asked the Internet naïve volunteers to practice Internet searching for an hour each day for about one week. This relatively brief training period led to significant increases in brain activation in neural circuits controlling working memory (very short-term learning and recall) and decision-making (Moody et al, 2009; Small & Vorgan, 2008).

So international headlines read "Google is Making Us Smart!" — a conclusion that seemed to contradict concerns that Google could be making us "stoopid" (Carr, 2008) — that is, too much technology may be curtailing our instinct to take the time to tackle issues in depth. Instead, we may be training our brains for fast-paced breadth of thinking as we develop a staccato-style of problem solving, jumping from idea to idea just as we dash from website to website.

Instead, we may be training our brains for fast-paced breadth of thinking as we develop a staccato-style of problem solving, jumping from idea to idea just as we dash from website to website.

This perpetual technology exposure may well be leading to the next major milestone in brain evolution (Small & Vorgan, 2008). Over 300,000 years ago, our ancestors discovered hand-held tools, which led to the co-evolution of language, goal-directed behavior, social networking and accelerated development of the frontal lobe, which controls these functions. Today, video-game-brain, Internet addiction and other technology side effects may be suppressing frontal lobe executive skills and our ability to communicate face-to-face. Instead, our brains are developing circuitry for online social networking and adapting to a new multitasking technology culture. A new study suggests that young people who spend too much time with text messaging may be sacrificing accuracy for expediency. One of the convenient features of our handheld devices — a program that figures out the word we want to use before we finish typing it — may be part of the problem. Abramson and colleagues (2009) studied over 300 children aged 11 to 14 and found that kids who used mobile phones performed faster on a battery of cognitive tests, but they also made significantly more errors. The bottom line is that frequent use of the devices makes kids fast and sloppy.

This is likely a problem for middle-aged and older digital immigrants as well. Today's rapid pace of information constantly assaulting our brains challenges our ability to pay full attention to any one thing. Our laptops and instant messages pressure us into quick responses that lead us to sacrifice detail and accuracy. Radio and television announcers speak in time-compressed sentences leaving us with mere ideas of what they have said. Many people are replacing depth and subtlety in their thinking with quick mental facts that only skim the surface. The mental clutter, noise and frequent interruptions that assail most of us further fuel this frenetic cognitive style.

Though we think we can get more done when we divide our attention and multitask, we are not necessarily being more efficient. Studies show that when our brains switch back and forth from one task to another, our neural circuits take a small break in between — a time-consuming process that reduces efficiency. It's not unlike closing down one computer program and booting up another — it takes a few moments. With each attention shift, the brain's frontal lobe executive centers must activate different neural circuits.

Dr. Gloria Mark and associates at the University of California, Irvine, studied the work habits of high-tech office employees and found that each worker spent an average of only 11 minutes per project. Every time a worker was distracted from a task, it took the worker 25 minutes to return to it. Such distractions and interruptions not only plague our work environments, but they also intrude upon our leisure and family time. The bottom line is that despite people's perception that they are doing more and at a faster pace when they multitask, the brain seems to work better when implementing a single sustained task, one at a time.

Some particular combinations of tasks, however, do appear to improve mental efficiency. This included performing a task while also listening to music. Neuroscientists have found that some surgeons perform stressful non-surgical laboratory tasks more quickly and with increased accuracy when listening to their preferred musical selections. Music appears to enhance the efficiency of those who work with their hands. Music and manual tasks activate completely different parts of the brain; thus, effective multitasking sometimes appears to involve disparate brain regions. However, if you are working while listening to music you do not like, it may be distracting and decrease the efficiency of your multitasking.

Our UCLA brain scan studies do suggest that computer technologies have physiological effects and potential benefits for middle-aged and older adults. Internet searching engages complicated brain activity, which may help exercise and improve brain function. Compared with traditional book reading, the Internet's wealth of choices requires that people make decisions about what to click on in order to pursue more information, an activity that exercises important cognitive circuits in the brain. Also, searching the Web appears to rapidly enhance brain circuitry in older adults, demonstrating that our brains remain flexible and can continue to learn as we grow older.

Multitasking has become a necessary skill of modern life, but we need to acknowledge the challenges and adapt accordingly. Several strategies can help, such as striving to stay on one task longer, and avoiding task switching whenever possible. We can also learn and build multitasking skills with practice.

New technology is certainly changing our lives. I'm convinced that it is also changing our brains in both positive and negative ways. Whether it makes people smart or stupid depends on the duration, content and context of its use. As we continue to work and play in a high-tech world, we need to balance our online time with more traditional offline activities so that we manage the technology and maintain our quality of life.

References
- Abramson MJ, Benke GP, Dimitriadis C, Inyang IO, Sim MR, Wolfe RS, Croft RJ. Mobile telephone use is associated with changes in cognitive function in young adolescents. *Bioelectromagnetics*, 2009 Jul 30. [Epub ahead of print]
- Bookheimer SY, Strojwas MH, Cohen MS, Saunders AM, Pericak-Vance MA, Mazziotta JC, Small GW. Patterns of brain activation in people at risk for Alzheimer's disease. *New England Journal of Medicine*, 2000;343:450-456.
- Carr N. Is Google making us stoopid? *Atlantic*, July 2008.
- Moody TD, Small GW, Gaddipati H, Bookheimer SY. Neural activaty patterns in older adults following Internet training. *Society for Neuroscience*, 2009
- Small GW, Bookheimer SY, Thompson PM, Cole GM, Huang S-C, Kepe V, Barrio JR. Current and future uses of neuroimaging for cognitively impaired patients. *Lancet Neurology*, 2008;7:161-172
- Small GW, Kepe V, Ercoli LM, Siddarth P, Miller K, Bookheimer SY, Lavretsky H, Burggren AC, Cole G, Vinters HV, Thompson PM, Huang S-C, Satyamurthy N, Phelps ME, Barrio JR. PET of brain amyloid and tau in mild cognitive impairment. *New England Journal of Medicine*, 2006;355;2652-2663
- Small GW, Moody TD, Siddarth P, Bookheimer SY. Your brain on Google: Patterns of cerebral activation during Internet searching. *American Journal of Geriatric Psychiatry*, 2009;17:116-126.

GROWING OLD OR LIVING LONG:
TAKE YOUR PICK

Laura L. Carstensen

T he 20th century witnessed two profound changes in regions
of the world where people are well-educated and science and
technology flourish: Life expectancy nearly doubled, and fertility rates fell dramatically. As a result, individuals and populations
are aging.

Virtually all educated people are aware of the graying of the
United States, yet relatively few are as aware of its implications for
science, technology and human culture. Longer life is a remarkable
achievement, but now we need to apply what we are learning
in the natural and social sciences to redesign human culture to
accommodate long lives. We need to find cures for Alzheimer's
disease and arthritis, develop technologies that render many age-
related frailties such as poor balance invisible in the way eyeglasses
now compensate for presbyopia, and begin seriously rethinking
cultural norms, including the timing of education and retirement.

Laura L. Carstensen, Ph.D., is a member of the Psychology Department at Stanford University, where she is also founding director of the Stanford Center on Longevity and the
Fairleigh S. Dickinson Jr. professor in public policy. For more than 20 years her research has
been supported by the National Institute on Aging, and in 2005 she was honored with a
MERIT award. Carstensen is best known for socioemotional selectivity theory, a life-span
theory of motivation. She is the author of the book *A Long, Bright Future*.

*This essay is excerpted from "Growing Old or Living Long" and is reprinted with
permission from* Issues in Science and Technology, *copyright by The University of Texas at
Dallas, Richardson, Texas.*

Longevity is the largely unexpected consequence of improvements in general living conditions. Genetically speaking, we are no smarter or heartier than our relatives were 10,000 years ago. Nonetheless, in practical terms we are more biologically fit than our great-grandparents. Robert Fogel and his colleague Dora Costa coined the term "technophysio evolution" to refer to improvements in biological functioning that are a consequence of technological advances. They point out that technologies developed mostly in the past century vastly improved the quality and sustainability of the food supply. Subsequent improvements in nutrition were so dramatic that average body size increased by 50 percent and life expectancy doubled. The working capacity of vital organs greatly improved. Breakthroughs in manufacturing, transportation, energy production and communications contributed further to improvements in biological functioning. Medical technology now enables full recovery from accidents or illnesses that were previously fatal or disabling.

Even technophysio evolution may be too narrow a term. Just as dramatic as the technologies are the acceptance and incorporation of the advances into everyday life. Not only was pasteurization discovered, it was implemented in entire populations. Not only were insights into the spread of disease observed in laboratories, community-wide efforts to dispose of waste were systematically undertaken. Not only was child development better understood, child labor laws prevented little ones from working long hours in unsafe conditions. Culture changed. Life expectancy increased because we built a world that is exquisitely attuned to the needs of young people.

Remember, however, that advances of the 20th century did not aim to increase longevity or alleviate the disabling conditions of later life. Longer life was the byproduct of better conditions for the young.

The challenge today is to build a world that is just as responsive to the needs of very old people as to the very young. The solutions must come from science and technology. Unlike evolution by natural selection, which operates across millennia, improvements in functioning due to technological advances can occur in a matter of years. In fact, given that the first of the 77 million Boomers turned 60 in 2006, there is no time to waste. To the extent that we effectively use science and technology to compensate for human frailties at advanced ages, the conversation under way in the nation changes from one about old age to one about long life, and this is a far more interesting and more productive conversation to have.

Human need is the basis for virtually all of science. If we rise to the challenge of an aging population by systematically applying science and technology to questions that improve quality of life in adulthood and old age, longer-lived populations will inspire breakthroughs in the social, physical and biological sciences that will improve the quality of life at all ages. Longevity science will reveal ways to improve learning from birth to advanced ages and to deter age-related slowing in cognitive processing. Longevity science will draw enormously on insights about individuals' genomic predispositions and the environmental conditions that trigger the onset of disease, as well as identifying genetic differences in individuals who appear resilient despite bad habits. Longevity science will help us understand how stress slowly but surely affects health. Most of the challenges of longer-lived populations will require interdisciplinary collaborations. Behavioral science must be a part of this process.

Unlike evolution by natural selection, which operates across millennia, improvements in functioning due to technological advances can occur in a matter of years.

A VERY BRIEF MAINTENANCE MANUAL FOR AGING MACHINERY

—————— Sherwin B. Nuland ——————

A gradual though very slow increase in life expectancy was observable during the course of the past two millennia for which reasonably dependable records are available. But following this long period and thanks to public health measures and the advent of modern biomedicine, an absolute surge of some 33 years took place in the 20th century; and bringing with it certain problems that had never required attention until recent decades. Stated as simply as possible: the primary predicament in which the current and coming generations of oldsters — and the society which must provide for their needs — find themselves is the preservation of the functioning of joints, bones, hearts and brains that are in the process of losing their ability to perform efficiently.

Long-term care institutions are already filled with men and women so incapacitated that they require help with the simplest of needs, such as toileting and dressing themselves. Many of them are demented. For every such institutionalized example of the frail elderly there is a multiple number living in their own or a relative's home. The economic cost is high, but the cost in suffering, not only for the elderly themselves but for their families, is even greater.

Sherwin B. Nuland, M.D. is clinical professor of surgery at Yale University, and a fellow of its Institution for Social and Policy Studies. He teaches bioethics and medical history to medical students and undergraduates. In addition to writing *The Art of Aging* in 2007, Nuland is the author of *How We Die,* which won the National Book Award, and has been translated into 27 languages, as well as having been a *New York Times* bestseller for 34 weeks.

Among the many ways in which science and medicine have attempted to approach the increasing spate of such problems has been the very straightforward one of carrying out detailed studies of the factors that actually determine the disabilities of the aged. Discarding theories based on unproven assumptions and replacing them with scientific precision, gerontologists are able to make recommendations that go far toward relieving, and in some cases markedly diminishing, the depredations of the years. One of the first steps in the process of change was the definitive evidence that physical frailty, and not disease itself or any named pathology, is the most important determinant of whether an elderly person can care for himself and remain a vital contributing member of the community. Study after study has confirmed this conclusion, perhaps best stated by a team of Dutch gerontologists in a 1997 paper published in *Science*, as follows: "In the oldest old, loss of muscle strength is the limiting factor for an individual's chances of living an independent life until death."

Such a statement would have no meaning were it not for the repeatedly demonstrated fact that it is far less difficult to markedly increase muscle strength among the aged — and in fact those in the middle years and younger — than had previously been thought. It has consistently been shown that strength can be almost doubled within six or eight weeks even in the oldest old (by definition, those over 85) merely through a supervised high-intensity weight training program. Increasing muscle mass means increasing activity and its accompanying increased stress on bones. Bone needs stressing forces to provide the stimulus to remain dense and strong, thereby fighting off osteoporosis. An added, though not entirely unexpected bonus for those who participate in such programs, is the welcome lowering of systolic blood pressure that often comes with it.

Being more active encourages people to a healthier lifestyle. An oft-quoted confirmation of such a statement is a study in which a large group of University of Pennsylvania alumni averaging 68 years of age at the beginning of a long period of observation were able to postpone disability by an average of 7.75 years by consistent exercise, avoiding cigarettes and maintaining a normal weight. The best type of exercise for such purposes is anaerobic — exercise in which the body incurs an oxygen debt, such as resistance training with weights. Aerobic exercises — jogging, swimming, pedaling real or stationary bikes, and the like — do wonders for the heart and lungs, and have the added advantage that they appear to reduce the normal age-related loss of brain tissue and improve cerebral functioning, but they are less effective in building muscle.

The best type of exercise for such purposes is anaerobic — exercise in which the body incurs an oxygen debt, such as resistance training with weights.

Obviously, improving muscle strength and perhaps other bodily functions such as blood pressure is only part of the answer to the losses incurred by a body beyond middle age — the brain needs plenty of attention as well. It is by now no secret that continued intellectual stimulation is the key to avoiding much of the ravaging dementia and the apathy that steals the minds of so many of the homebound and institutionalized elderly. Granted, all the reading and museum-going in the world are not likely to reduce the incidence of strokes, both large and small, but such activities maintain the health of the connections between nerve cells — the synapses — and probably encourage the development of new brain cells regardless of age. They seem to do so by increasing the brain's production of any of a class of protein substances that have the ability to stimulate, strengthen and nourish new synapses in the brain, and encourage the appearance of new neurons, or nerve cells.

The production and effectiveness of such substances, called neurotrophic (nerve growth) factors, is determined by the amount of activity going on in nearby neural circuits: the more the circuits are used, the more neurotrophic factor is produced. This means not only that lost, damaged or impaired nerve cells can be replaced, but also that an increased population of new neurons may occur in certain locations in the brain, all due to challenging oneself mentally. Aerobic fitness exercises have been demonstrated to have a similar effect. They elevate the levels of brain-derived neurotrophic factor (BDNF, as the researchers call it), which acts to increase the number of synapses, promote the development of new capillaries in the brain, and protect nerve cells against the damage being caused by free radicals; in addition to the possibility that BDNF may encourage the development of new neurons from adult stem cells.

Such findings need to be snatched up by people of all ages. Those of us who are getting on in years, in particular, should snatch them up and run with them, literally. Vigorous exercise of mind and body is the key to prolonged independence and increased longevity. The well-known admonition of the recently departed popular sage, Ann Landers, says it all: "Use it or lose it."

THE $1 BILLION MISUNDERSTANDING

Leonard Hayflick

Modern research on the fundamental biology of aging began about 50 years ago when the enormous advances made in molecular and cell biology were thought to be capable of providing new insights into aging — then the most intractable aspect of human biology.

In the last few years the fundamental biology of aging has become broadly understood, not because of some spectacular discovery, but because of the slow realization that fundamental laws of physics — once thought not to apply to living forms — in fact, do apply.

A half-century was required to reach this understanding because of failures by research policymakers and scientists themselves who have failed to distinguish aging from its' associated diseases and from the determinants of longevity. This has been compounded by the wide spectrum of divergent meanings given to the rubric "research

Leonard Hayflick, Ph.D. is professor of anatomy at the University of California, San Francisco. He is a past president of the Gerontological Society of America, former editor-in-chief of *Experimental Gerontology*, and currently an academician of the Ukrainian Academy of Medical Sciences and a corresponding member of the Société de Biologie of France. Hayflick discovered that cultured normal human cells are mortal and have a limited capacity for replication and that cancer cells are immortal. He also isolated and identified the etiological agent of primary atypical pneumonia (*Mycoplasma pneumoniae*). His normal human cell strain WI-38 has been used to produce most of the world's human virus vaccines benefitting over two billion people. He also authored the popular book, *How and Why We Age*, which has been translated into nine languages and was a selection of The Book-of-the-Month Club.

on aging." Regrettably, these failures continue and explain why our understanding of the fundamental biology of aging is explicable only in its broadest terms. Not only has this situation crippled efforts to better understand the aging process, it also has deceived many into wrongly believing that enormous progress is being made.

To understand why progress continues to be slow is the need to define the four aspects of the finitude of life: aging, longevity determination, age-associated diseases and (not to be considered here) death.

Aging

Age changes can occur in only two fundamental ways: either by a purposeful program driven by genes or by stochastic or random events.

It is a cornerstone of modern biology that a purposeful genetic program drives all biological processes that occur from conception to reproductive maturation. But, once reproductive maturation is reached, thought is divided in respect to whether the aging process results from a continuation of the genetic program or whether it occurs by the accumulation of dysfunctional molecules. Yet, there is no direct evidence that genes drive age changes—a claim made because of the failure to distinguish age changes from longevity determinants.

The aging phenotype is expressed after reproductive maturation and is driven by random events in animals that reach a fixed size in adulthood. No gene that codes for a universal biomarker of aging has been found. Analogously, inanimate objects also require no instructions to age. Evidence for the belief that aging is a random or stochastic process is that: 1) everything in the universe changes or ages in space-time without being driven by a purposeful program; 2) there is no direct evidence that age changes are governed by a genetic program; and 3) there is a huge body of knowledge indicating that age changes are characterized by the accumulation of dysfunctional molecules.

The common denominator that underlies all causes of aging is change in molecular structure and, hence, in function. It is caused by the intrinsic thermodynamic instability of complex biomolecules, or the manifestations of the Second Law of Thermodynamics. Entropy increase was, until recently, dismissed as a cause of biological aging because biological systems are open. The recent re-interpretation of the Second Law states that "Entropy is the tendency for concentrated energy to disperse when unhindered regardless of whether the system is open or closed. The 'hindrance' is the relative strength of chemical bonds."

Thus, biological aging can be defined as the random, systemic accumulation of dysfunctional molecules that exceeds repair capacity.

The prevention of chemical bond breakage until reproductive maturation is the *sine qua non* for the maintenance of life and species continuity. This is the role of longevity determinants or maintenance systems that ultimately also suffer the same effects of the Second Law as do their substrate molecules.

Thus, biological aging can be defined as the random, systemic accumulation of dysfunctional molecules that exceeds repair capacity. These occur throughout life, but in youth the balance favors the bodies' enormous capacity for repair, turnover and synthesis; otherwise individuals would not live long enough to reproduce and the species would vanish. After reproductive maturation the balance shifts toward irreparable, dysfunctional molecules, including those that compose the maintenance systems themselves. Then the myriad decrements that produce the aging phenotype are revealed. This accumulation of dysfunctional molecules increases vulnerability to age-associated diseases.

Blueprints contain no information instructing a car how to age, yet in their absence molecules composing the car dissipate energy producing structural and functional losses. Analogously, the genome also does not contain instructions for aging because, like the car, instructions are unnecessary to drive a spontaneous process.

Longevity Determination

The second aspect of the finitude of life is longevity determination — a completely different process from aging.

Longevity is determined by the length of time that the synthesis, turnover and repair processes can maintain the biologically active state of their substrate molecules. This process is governed by the genome.

Unlike the stochastic process that characterizes aging, longevity determination is not a random process. It is governed by the enormous excess of physiological reserve produced until the time of reproductive maturation and evolved through natural selection to better guarantee survival to that age. Thus, the determination of longevity is incidental to the main goal of the genome, which is to reach reproductive maturity.

Longevity determination is an entirely different process from aging and is independent of it. One might think of longevity determination as the energy state of molecules before they incur age changes. This energy state addresses the question: "Why do we live as long as we do?"

One might think of aging as the state of molecules after they have incurred irreparable damage leading to the aging phenotype. This condition addresses the question: "Why do things eventually change or go wrong?"

Aging is a catabolic process that is chance driven. Longevity determination is an anabolic process that, indirectly, is genome driven. They are opposing forces.

The genome directs events until reproductive maturation after which the aging process dominates. Thus, the genome only indirectly determines potential longevity by governing the levels of excess physiological capacity, repair and turnover. No specific genes determine longevity but, collectively, they all govern aspects of biological processes that increase the likelihood of survival to reproductive maturity. The variations in excess physiological capacity, repair and turnover account for the differences found in longevity both within and between species.

> **Aging is a catabolic process that is chance driven. Longevity determination is an anabolic process that, indirectly, is genome driven. They are opposing forces.**

The many studies with invertebrates that have led to the view that genes are involved in aging have not revealed a reversal or arrest of the inexorable expression of dysfunctional molecules that is the hallmark of aging. Where these studies have revealed greater longevities, it is because the determinants of longevity have been manipulated well before the aging process begins. None of these studies using invertebrates has demonstrated that the manipulation of genes has slowed, stopped or reversed the aging process. Experiments on invertebrate "aging" usually have as their end point all causes of mortality. That end point tells us nothing directly about aging. It can tell us something about longevity determinants.

Age-associated Diseases

The third, and last of the four aspects, of the finitude of life to be discussed is age-associated diseases. The distinction between the aging process and age-associated disease is rooted in several practical observations:

Unlike any disease, age changes: 1) occur in every metazoan that reaches a fixed size in adulthood; 2) cross virtually all species barriers; 3) occur in all members of a species only after the age of reproductive maturation; 4) occur in all animals protected by humans even when that species probably has not experienced aging for thousands or even millions of years; 5) occur in virtually all animate and inanimate objects; and 6) have the same universal molecular etiology, that is, thermodynamic instability.

There is no disease or pathology that has all of these properties.

The key question is: "Why are old cells more vulnerable to pathology than are young cells?"

What is Research on Aging?

The second contributor to our failure to make significant progress in understanding the fundamental biology of aging is use of the term "aging research" or, more properly, "research on aging."

Research on aging embraces all aspects of the finitude of life, only one small part of which is the study of the fundamental biology of aging.

The common belief—held especially by policymakers and funding agencies—is that supporting "Aging Research" includes research on age-associated diseases whose resolution will somehow provide insights into the fundamental biology of aging. It will not.

No successes in geriatric medicine will provide insight into the fundamental biology of aging. To believe that it will, is the basis for the present $1 billion misunderstanding, which is what is spent in the belief that disease or pathology resolution will result in understanding the etiology of age changes. It will not, for the same reasons that the resolution of childhood diseases, like Wilm's tumors, iron deficiency anemia, measles and poliomyelitis did not increase our understanding of childhood development.

The spurious belief that controlling age-associated pathologies will provide insight into the fundamental aging processes, ironically, is contradicted by another common, but accurate, belief in medicine. It is the dogma that "The greatest risk factor for the leading causes of death is the aging process."

The irony is that it does not require a great leap of intellect to ask: "Then, why is the funding for research on the fundamental biology of aging infinitesimal when compared to the funding for research on the leading causes of death?"

WHY DO ANTI-AGING DOCTORS DIE?

———— S. Jay Olshansky ————

B oastful claims of miracle cures for just about every disease that has plagued humanity have been part of folklore dating back thousands of years. Hucksterism has taken on many forms over the centuries. Ancient Egyptians claimed miracle balms would restore youthful appearance. Chinese and Indian sages asserted that death could be forestalled by controlling how rapidly we breathe. Alchemists from the middle ages concocted "scientific" potions to combat diseases. Physicians in the early 20th century grafted the glands from animals onto older men with claims of rejuvenation, while modern equivalents with impressive degrees following their names assert that immortality is within reach.

With a rapidly aging population now facing old age with a defiant attitude and money in their pockets, anti-aging "medicine" — the modern version of alchemy — has become popular once again. Ironically, those now proclaiming to be the modern prophets of this ancient ruse boast that they invented the idea. The hucksters

S. Jay Olshansky, Ph.D. is a professor in the School of Public Health at the University of Illinois at Chicago, and a research associate at the Center on Aging at the University of Chicago and at the London School of Hygiene and Tropical Medicine. The focus of his research to date has been on estimates of the upper limits to human longevity, exploring the health and public policy implications associated with individual and population aging; forecasts of the size, survival and age structure of the population; pursuit of the scientific means to slow aging in people ("The Longevity Dividend"); and global implications of the re-emergence of infectious and parasitic diseases. Olshansky is the first author of *The Quest for Immortality: Science at the Frontiers of Aging.*

evidently have no sense of history ... or shame. If any of these declarations were actually true, there would be no disease, no aging and no death. The fact that all three are still with us has not deterred the true believers throughout the centuries, all of whom share one common characteristic beyond their collective fantasy: they are all dead. The hucksters have taken on new and more interesting forms in recent years, and they are still working hard to separate us from our money.

The hucksters evidently have no sense of history ... or shame. If any of these declarations were actually true, there would be no disease, no aging and no death.

These observations lead to one obvious question that all consumers of health products should be asking: Why Do Anti-Aging Doctors Die? I mean no disrespect to those who have passed away; and this is but a very short list among many who could be mentioned. But perhaps the time has arrived for a reality check. Not everyone on the following list is an actual doctor, but in the end that doesn't matter. For even those who claim to have advanced degrees can easily obtain them without actually going to school.

Pre 20th Century

Ko Hung—born in 283, died in 343 at age 60. Claimed immortality is possible by reducing intake of food and ingesting certain substances. *Roger Bacon*—born in 1214, died in 1292 at age 78. Claimed immortality is possible by adopting "secret arts of the past" (i.e., lifestyles of the ancient patriarchs).

Luigi Cornaro — born in 1467, died in 1566 at age 98. Advocated caloric restriction.

Eugen Steinach — born in 1861, died in 1944 at age 83. Claimed aging could be reversed and sexual function restored with a vasectomy — a precursor to the hormone theory of aging.

Jerome I. Rodale — born in 1898, died in 1971 at age 72. Advocate for organic foods and founder of *Prevention Magazine* — cause of death, heart attack.

20th and 21st Centuries

Linus Pauling — born in 1901, died in 1994 at age 93. Claimed that high doses of vitamin C (which he used) would prevent colds and cancer — cause of death, cancer.

William Regelson — born in 1926, died in 2002 at age 76. Claimed DHEA (which he used) is an anti-aging hormone.

Roy Walford — born in 1924, died in 2004 at age 79. Claimed caloric restriction (which he followed) would lead us all to live to 120 — cause of death, ALS.

Alan Mintz — born in 1938, died in 2007 at age 69. Claimed growth hormone (which he used) reverses aging — cause of death, possible brain tumor.

William Constitution O'Rights (aka "The First Immortal") — born in 1966, died in 2009 at age 43. Member of the Immortality Institute — died from small cell lung carcinoma and smoked cigarettes right up until the time of his death.

The sobering answer to the question of this essay is that anti-aging doctors and other advocates for radical life extension die; and they have done so for the same reasons as everyone else at about the same ages. In spite of boastful (and often profitable) claims to the contrary, they have aged, grown old, their bodies failed, they acquired disease, and they have all eventually succumbed to the ravages of time. In short, they have been less than truthful to consumers of public health. Still their numbers are growing.

Having burst the bubble of the past and present anti-aging "medicine" movement, I cannot end this essay without telling you the most important news of all. Although there are no magical potions that exist today that can even come close to fulfilling the claims of immortalists past and present, scientists are on the verge of breakthroughs that may enable many of us today to drink from a modest equivalent of a fountain of youth. The scientific study of aging is at an exciting precipice, with new evidence emerging daily about successful research efforts to extend life and slow aging in other species. Although immortality or radical life extension may not be in the cards for the readers of this essay, the time may come soon when the means to make us healthier for a longer period of time will become readily available. We should all be happy with that ... for the alternative has not changed.

COMBAT AGEISM TO FIGHT AGE-RELATED NEURODEGENERATION

⊢──────── Bruce L. Miller, M.D. ────────⊣

T oday's world is quite different from the world we knew as little as 50 years ago. Strides in technology and public health, along with changing socio-economic factors, have had a profound effect on longevity. We enjoy greater life expectancy than ever before, and as a result, people over 60 years old represent the fastest growing age group worldwide. Put simply, the human population is aging.

These extra years are valuable; they represent unprecedented opportunity for elders to share their wisdom and experience with members of the younger generation. Wisdom is an attribute that, almost by definition, improves with aging. It is no accident that many of us look to our parents and grandparents for advice on our most difficult problems. It is their cumulative experience — generated across the lifespan — that gives the elderly special value for any society.

Yet aging is an important risk factor associated with myriad health problems. The risk of neurodegenerative disorders increases dramatically as we get older, in the case of Alzheimer's disease, doubling every five years after the age of 65. These conditions have

Bruce L. Miller, M.D. is director of the Memory and Aging Center at the University of California, San Francisco School of Medicine; and an A.W. and Mary Margaret Clausen Distinguished Professor of neurology and psychiatry in the School's Department of Neurology. He also is the author of more than 400 publications, including the recent books, *The Behavioral Neurology of Dementia* and *The Human Frontal Lobes*.

a devastating impact on the lives of patients and their loved ones and place a huge burden on healthcare infrastructures and society as a whole. Uncovering the biological mechanisms underlying these conditions and developing treatments will be necessary if we are to continue to see the elderly as a gift — not a burden.

As the genes, proteins and molecular mechanisms behind these diseases are discovered, we are increasingly moving toward highly targeted therapeutics to overcome each of the neurodegenerative conditions that underlie unhealthy cognitive aging. Nevertheless, this is a long process, with cures rarely revealed overnight. Rather, progress often comes first in the form of increasingly effective management and treatments to slow or halt further decline — all important goals in their own right. So while hopes for effective treatments are well-founded, science and technology can move only so fast. While we wait for research and medicine to catch up, surely we should not waste our early opportunities with this new, older, global population. Might there be something we can do to ease this transition and welcome this new era of prolonged life?

Dismissed, scorned, ridiculed, or even feared, some people entering their twilight years lose all contact with people from younger generations. What an incredible loss to society!

As age-related neurodegenerative diseases are inextricably intertwined with our concept of what defines "who" a person is — memories, personality, emotions, intellect — so too are our attitudes towards the aging process and members of the older generation. Common misconceptions and prejudices all too often lead to underestimation and dehumanization of our elders. It seems too easy to forget that these are the people we will eventually become. Dismissed, scorned, ridiculed, or even feared, some people entering their twilight years lose all contact with people from younger generations. What an incredible loss to society! Far from reaping the benefits of the institutional memory preserved in those who live long into their old age, it seems we prefer them forgotten.

We must critically examine our attitude towards aging. Successful societies understand that the old are an invaluable resource and their wisdom is recognized, even institutionalized, as part of social, political and religious philosophies. History abounds with great writers, artists, businessmen, and religious and social leaders who were over 70. William Yeats, George Bernard Shaw, Henri Matisse, Pablo Picasso, Mahatma Gandhi and Golda Meir all accomplished incredible feats well into their old age, demonstrating how valuable our elders are to society.

It is undeniable that even normal aging is associated with mild declines in cognitive function, and gradual physical deterioration. Fewer people are aware of a growing body of evidence that some functions actually *improve* as we age.

When compared to younger adults, older individuals have a greater ability to regulate their emotions and are more readily able to find effective strategies for solving highly emotional problems like interpersonal conflicts. As people grow older they accumulate more knowledge and understanding of the world, the nature of conflict, the personalities of the people around them, and insights into which social strategies are most beneficial. Also, it has been proposed that as people age, they become aware of their limited time and reassess their priorities — with emotional well-being taking a prominent role. To achieve this goal, more attention is devoted to the positive aspects of life, and that which is negative is suppressed or avoided. This focus on the positive also lends itself to increased resilience — a capacity to bounce back from difficulties. Astonishingly, while we know that aging is accompanied by cognitive decline, older adults are able to maintain their cognitive functions in the face of demands to regulate themselves following an emotional distraction, while their younger counterparts experience significant impairment.

Creativity is another frequently overlooked aspect of the aging process, and may flourish even in the context of neurodegenerative disorders. Patients with progressive aphasia sometimes experience a new-found interest in music or visual art, and become extremely productive and talented even as their disease progresses. Composer Maurice Ravel continued to conceive musical works even after his ability to read music had failed due to progressive aphasia. Even for patients suffering from Alzheimer's disease, a disorder in which visuospatial difficulties are prominent, artwork may become less realistic, but no less artistically skilled in the use of color and form, as is exemplified by the works of Willem de Kooning. And social skills may be preserved, or even enhanced in many patients in the early stages of Alzheimer's disease. Great works were produced by playwright Eugene O'Neill against a background of Parkinson's disease.

In seeing our elders in this new, positive light, might we as a society finally realize the value of old age? Can we come to accept, or even welcome, the fact that this is the inevitable destination of our journey through life? Such recognition will bring countless advantages: eradication of the loneliness currently so prevalent in old age; discovery of cultural, intellectual and emotional contributions that our elders have to offer society; and perhaps most importantly, motivation for younger people to take early action in preparation for enjoyment of later life. Living life with an awareness and appreciation for old age will foster a desire to protect ourselves from risk factors associated with cognitive decline and dementia. This involves taking steps toward reducing vascular risk factors (like hypertension, obesity, smoking, diabetes and cholesterol), and addressing possible psychiatric risk factors like depression.

A healthy old age — with the growth of these long-awaited qualities of emotional control, social flexibility, creativity, wisdom, optimism and resilience — is something to which we should aspire. Those in whom we already recognize these qualities should be celebrated. In this way, the changing face of our aging demographic can be greeted by a more thoughtful, dignified and appreciative society. 🔘

Further reading
- Seeley WW, Matthews BR, Crawford RK, Gorno-Tempini ML, Foti D, Mackenzie IR, Miller BL. "Unravelling Boléro: progressive aphasia, transmodal creativity and the right posterior neocortex." *Brain.* 2008 Jan;131(Pt 1):39-49. Epub 2007 Dec 5.
- Sturm VE, Rosen HJ, Allison S, Miller BL, Levenson RW. "Self-conscious emotion deficits in frontotemporal lobar degeneration." *Brain.* 2006 Sep;129(Pt 9):2508-16. Epub 2006 Jul 14.

HOW CAN WE ENSURE QUALITY WITH EXTENDED LIFE EXPECTANCY?

Aubrey D.N.J. de Grey

t is often noted that life expectancy roughly doubled during the 20th century, but that statistic is an unhelpful merger of two phases. Until roughly World War II, gains were achieved mostly via a progressive lowering of mortality rates in infancy and childbirth; thereafter, by contrast, the ages at which the most progress has been made are middle-age and above. Most observers predict that these more recent gains, which have averaged roughly two years per decade, will continue for some time, subject only to appropriate public health measures to curtail the rise in obesity and its associated diseases.

This success in postponing death from age-related causes has been something of a mixed blessing. The average age until which people remain relatively free of age-related ill-health has also risen, by an amount comparable to the rise in average longevity. But when specific age-related diseases are considered individually, the picture

Aubrey D.N.J. de Grey, Ph.D. is a biomedical gerontologist based in Cambridge, United Kingdom, and is the chief science officer of SENS Foundation, a nonprofit charity dedicated to combating the aging process. He is also editor-in-chief of *Rejuvenation Research*, the world's highest-impact peer-reviewed journal focused on intervention in aging. His research interests encompass the causes of all the accumulating and eventually pathogenic molecular and cellular side-effects of metabolism ("damage") that constitute mammalian aging and the design of interventions to repair and/or obviate that damage. He has developed a possibly comprehensive plan for such repair, termed "Strategies for Engineered Negligible Senescence" (SENS), which breaks aging down into seven major classes of damage and identifies detailed approaches to addressing each one.

is mixed: the average age of survival with cardiovascular disease has diminished, while for Alzheimer's and cancer it has risen.

The economic benefits of postponing age-related ill-health and death are also mixed. It has been estimated that progress against age-related diseases has enormously benefited the economies of the industrialized world over the past 50 years — due to an increase in the proportion of individuals who are net contributors to national wealth rather than consumers of it. However, because the age at which people retire has not remotely kept pace with rising life expectancy, the proportion of the population who are receiving pensions and related benefits has also risen, with the result that a major crisis of pension plans in both the private and public sector is looming. This problem is exacerbated in the short term by the "baby boom," the sharp (albeit temporary) rise in the birth rate in the United States and elsewhere following World War II, which is just about to start feeding through into the pension system.

Therefore, considerable challenges are facing the world's major economies in regard to maintaining elderly people's quality of life in the coming decades. How can these challenges best be addressed? Several options must be considered.

Without doubt, there will continue to be immense value in pursuing new ways to postpone the onset and progression of the major age-related diseases, especially those with a long survival time (such as Alzheimer's disease). These diseases sharply diminish the quality of life of both sufferers and their loved ones, and the financial cost of caring for sufferers impacts the quality of life of the whole of society.

In principle, any economic benefit accruing from postponing age-related ill-health could be considerably increased if such therapies did not similarly postpone death. This concept, generally

described using the term "compression of morbidity," has been en-
ergetically championed by biogerontologists for the past 30 years.
However, such an argument is decidedly dubious. First of all, there
is no evidence that therapies which postpone age-related ill-health,
but do not extend longevity by a comparable amount, are feasible.
It is intuitively much more likely that the period of ill-health will be
shifted to a greater age, but not shortened.
Second, it is not at all clear — indeed, arguably
the opposite is clear — that the public wish for
a compression of morbidity. There seems to
be unequivocal support for interventions that
keep the frail and sick elderly alive, in fact.

> **Regenerative medicine has the crucial advantage that it actually reverses age-related decline, rather than merely retarding it.**

However, a robust reason for optimism
about the impact of increasing our lifespan
exists. It arises from the impressive and
ever-accelerating progress being seen in
regenerative medicine, which is fast reaching
a level of sophistication that will allow it to
be applied to the immensely multi-faceted
problem of aging. Regenerative medicine
has the crucial advantage that it actually reverses age-related
decline, rather than merely retarding it. The demographic, and thus
economic, impact of that feature can hardly be overstated.

To see this, we must consider the relationship between the
average proportion of one's life that is spent in ill-health at the end
of life and the proportion of people in that condition at any given
instant. In a world where no progress is being made in postponing
either age-related ill-health or death, these proportions are clearly
equal. But when progress is occurring, a sort of Doppler effect
emerges, whereby the latter proportion is smaller than the former.

And unlike the auditory Doppler effect, in this case the relationship is asymptotic: There is a finite rate of progress in postponing aging beyond which no one is in a state of age-related ill-health. That rate is, of course, one year per year — only a few times what we are achieving already.

It is, however, crucial to bear in mind that preventative therapies exhibit a lag between their onset and their beneficial consequences. Accordingly, even if we were to develop therapies that postponed aging when begun in childhood, and we improved those therapies faster than one year of postponement per year, those unfortunates who are already too old to benefit from the therapies would remain in (or would enter) age-related ill-health just as before.

Thus, the ideal therapies, in terms of both quality of life and economic benefit, are without doubt regenerative interventions that benefit those who are already experiencing, or at least approaching, the decrepitude and disease of old age. Such interventions would reduce the number of such sufferers more rapidly than any other type of treatment, and the economic impact would be correspondingly more severe and more rapid.

The sole question remaining, therefore, is this: Are such interventions feasible in the foreseeable future? In my view, they almost certainly are. Regenerative medicine is arguably the most burgeoning field in the whole of biomedicine at present, with progress on all fronts occurring by leaps and bounds. In large part, the foundations for applying it to aging are already in place or imminent. It also remains to combine those therapies (which will inevitably be piecemeal) into a sufficiently comprehensive panel to span all the pathways by which lifelong accumulating molecular and cellular damage eventually causes age-related decline. The time to start addressing these challenges in earnest is now.

SOCIETAL

CAREGIVING'S TRANSFORMATIVE INFLUENCE ON AN AGING AMERICA

Larry D. Wright, M.D., A.G.S.F.

Caregiving for older adults with declining health and functional status is almost certain to become one of America's greatest challenges of the 21st century. Effectively addressing the issues it presents may require a cultural paradigm shift that could have a transformative influence on how our society progresses.

If such statements seem exaggerated, consider the context in which the caregiving challenge arises. Demographic projections for progressive aging of the U.S. population during the first half of this century are well documented and compelling. The overall number Americans reaching retirement age will more than double while those over 85 years — the cohort with the highest rates of chronic disease, frailty and dependency — will grow by approximately five times the current number.

Today, the United States and many western nations seem mired in a very unhealthy perspective marked by extreme glorification of all things youthful, coupled with extraordinary aversion to and denial

Larry D. Wright, M.D., A.G.S.F. is director of the Schmieding Center for Senior Health and Education, a regional program of the Reynolds Institute on Aging at the University of Arkansas for Medical Sciences. His position includes directing the Center's nationally acclaimed Home Caregiver Training program. With more than 30 years of community based practice in geriatric medicine, he also is an associate professor in the UAMS Reynolds Department of Geriatrics and medical director of senior health services for Northwest Health Systems.

of aging. Most Americans are unsure how they feel about their own aging or about the aging of our society.

The gift of 30 additional years of life expectancy over the past century seems a mixed blessing at best. The potential reward of extended retirement loses some of its appeal when considered along with the list of apparent negatives including rising healthcare costs, the demands of increasing dependency and the indignities associated with the pervasive ageism of our youth-oriented culture.

Add to that the inadequacies of the current long-term care system and the negative perception of nursing homes, along with the strong preference of most older adults to remain in their homes — even as chronic diseases lead to progressive frailty and dependency — and you have a recipe for depression ... if not despair.

Looming over the next two decades is the even harsher reality of major workforce shortages in long-term care, which may guarantee that high quality care cannot be delivered, even if system reforms are implemented.

Even before the demographic surge of Boomers begins to swell the retirement ranks, the reality of a broken system for providing long-term care is increasingly apparent. It is a system that promises too little and delivers even less. Looming over the next two decades is the even harsher reality of major workforce shortages in long-term care, which may guarantee that high quality care cannot be delivered, even if system reforms are implemented.

A prominent factor in the present reality is a significant shortage of direct care workers, especially available caregivers who can be hired by elders and their families to work in the home setting. The

Institute on Medicine's 2008 report on the workforce challenges of an aging America emphasized the need to recruit, train and retain these frontline caregivers to be ready for the aging tsunami that is coming. It recommended setting strong national standards of training for these workers who currently require little or no formal training in most states.

According to the 2002 "Health and Retirement Study," approximately 8.7 million elders in the United States are receiving long-term care in the home — as defined by the need for assistance with at least one activity of daily living (ADL). Of those, 2 million are classified as severely disabled or having three or more areas of ADL dependency. To put that in perspective, the total population of elders receiving long-term care in nursing homes was estimated to be 1.7 million in 2002 and has fallen to approximately 1.4 million currently.

Not only are most older Americans who need long-term care receiving it at home, it is no surprise that the overwhelming majority prefer to remain at home for care no matter how dependent or disabled they may become. Recent Census Bureau data show the percentage of adults 75 and older living in nursing homes has declined significantly during the past decade and a half, from 10.2 percent in 1990 to 7.4 percent in 2006. Even the oldest-old are less likely to reside in nursing homes now: 16 percent of adults over 85 now live in nursing homes compared to 21 percent in 1985, according to the "National Nursing Home Survey."

Unfortunately for frail elders, the long recognized observation is still true that the single most important determinant of whether one will have to move to a nursing home is the presence or absence of an adult female relative willing to serve as primary caregiver. The reality of just how much family caregivers can be relied on in the future may change quite a bit as the demographic trends in the elderly population and the changing make up of the American family make it much less likely that a family caregiver will be available.

The "informal caregiver workforce," a euphemism for unpaid family and other volunteer caregivers, provides 75-80 percent of the care for older adults in the home. By any standards, this represents a huge contribution to long-term care in this country. But in economic terms, it has been variously estimated that this unpaid care in the home saves $196 billion to more than $300 billion annually to the American economy. Without some types of formal support for these family caregivers (e.g. tax relief or social security credit for work at home, etc.), this huge contribution will be threatened.

There is a mounting consensus among the professional health-care and social services communities favoring a thoughtful but comprehensive overhaul of the long-term care system in the United States. In fact, strange as it may sound, reaching agreement on how to change the long-term care system would likely be much less difficult than implementing such systemic change.

If financing the new system were removed from the discussion momentarily, arguably the biggest obstacle would be workforce shortages. The most challenging of these would undoubtedly be the inadequate number of frontline caregivers (personal care assistants and nurse assistants) to provide in-home care for the functionally dependent elderly. And the great majority of these paid workers have had minimal, if any, formal training in caring for elders at home.

Any such rational reorientation of the system would result in a new emphasis on care in the home as part of a more integrated system in which care, and reimbursement of care, follows the patient rather than being unreasonably restricted to the institutional setting, as is the current reality. Clearly the majority of long-term care already occurs in the home. The description of the current long-term care system as being "institution centered" reflects the system's emphasis and bias with respect to regulatory standards of care, reimbursement and entitlement.

With the disproportionate numbers of individuals receiving their care at home, it is ironic that most of this care seems to occur outside the system rather than within an integrated system. By this I mean that caregivers paid privately by families legally fly under the radar that monitors standards of training and care for the public system. This reality is largely true whether such caregivers work for a commercial home care agency (non-medical) or are working as independent contractors.

The inadequacy of the long-term care system to satisfactorily meet the current and projected demands for the burgeoning elder population is increasingly more evident. What may only become apparent later is the less accepting attitude of future elders, the so-called "Age Boomers," toward the limited options offered by the system to deliver the care they most need and desire when they begin to lose their independence.

In particular, it is almost certain that future retirees will not find the current institutional bias to be satisfactory and will be even more insistent on receiving needed care in the home setting. Those most needing long-term care services now, the World War II generation, though often displeased with this

> **What may only become apparent later is the less accepting attitude of future elders, the so-called "Age Boomers," toward the limited options offered by the system to deliver the care they most need and desire when they begin to lose their independence.**

aspect of care delivery, have been reluctant to complain. At the risk of stereotyping, it does seem that among the many cited virtues of the "Greatest Generation" has been its sacrificial willingness to accept the undesirable rather than risk "being a burden" to family or society.

Predictably this will not be a feature of Boomers' late-life personality. And on this point, Boomers' attitudes may serve their generation and broader society well. Boomers' political capital may prove to be sufficient clout to accomplish the desperately needed reform of the long-term care system. If so, it likely will result from their initial exposure to the limitations of the system and the demands of caregiving they learn while coping with caring for their own aging parents.

As critically important as overhaul of the long-term care system is for this country, there is an even more important reason for making elder caregiving a national priority. Psychologically, and perhaps spiritually, as a culture we must rid ourselves of the scourge of ageism that segregates and alienates us from one another.

We desperately need to develop a new age-integrated concept of healthy interdependence. It begins with rediscovering the primal underpinnings of intergenerational community life: respect for the entirety of the aging process and mutual respect amongst generations. The positive impact of this fundamental transformation will positively affect the elders receiving care as well the younger adult caregivers.

All things considered, it is possible that this most noble human endeavor of caregiving could serve as the path toward a more humane society.

EXPLOITING TECHNOLOGY AND COLLABORATIVE INNOVATION TO ENABLE QUALITY AGING

—— Joseph F. Coughlin ——

A ging is not for wimps. While living longer has become remarkably commonplace, living well takes a lot of work. Longevity is creating new and expanded "jobs" for individuals, families, formal caregivers and public agencies. During the past decade many have argued that technology is the answer to aging — without really asking what the question is. This definition of the "aging and technology opportunity" is driven by those who are wildly passionate about invention, but not fluent in the art of innovation — that is, putting ideas to practical use. The questions that should be asked by policymakers, business and the aging community are:

- What are the jobs of aging services that we are trying to achieve?
- How might technology and collaborative partnerships accomplish these tasks or produce superior outcomes?
- Where should policymakers and business direct their limited resources to creatively exploit technology to enable individuals and families to live better — not just longer?

Understanding the Job(s) of Longevity

Real innovations are policies, products and services that respond to the jobs of the consumer or end user. What are the jobs of longevity?

Joseph F. Coughlin, Ph.D. is the founder and director of the Massachusetts Institute of Technology AgeLab (http://agelab.mit.edu). Based in MIT's Engineering Systems Division, Coughlin teaches policy and strategic management.

They look a lot like what we do in our younger years but become far more critical, diverse, complex, fragile, and as health declines, more out of our personal control.

There is a long list of jobs that support living longer. They begin at the very base of Maslow's oft-cited "needs" pyramid beginning with safety, security, food and shelter. In the middle there is social engagement, contribution and even play. At the top, where some have the good fortune to be concerned, is meaning and personal legacy. The jobs of longevity require the precision of a tax accountant, the coordination skills of an appointment secretary, and the discipline of a marathon runner.

The jobs of longevity require the precision of a tax accountant, the coordination skills of an appointment secretary, and the discipline of a marathon runner.

Consider just a few common and critical examples. Staying in your home can become an extreme sport in old age. A light bulb that you have changed many times before now seems just high enough to make using a ladder a serious hazard. Who does an older adult, or their family, trust to go into the home and do routine maintenance, cleaning and repairs?

Once an occasion to look forward to, dinner is now both exhausting to prepare and lonely to partake in. The basic tasks of shopping, transporting and finally "putting away" the groceries can become barriers to good nutrition, wellbeing and eventually independence.

Transportation works so well for nearly everyone that, like electricity, it is never thought of until it is not available. Driving is overwhelmingly the preferred mode of transportation for most Americans. Yet, over time, an older person may lose their confidence or capacity to drive safely. More than mobility is lost when driving stops — for the more than 70 percent of Americans over age 50 who live in the suburbs or rural areas where transit is scarce — their very connection to life is severed.

Managing health is a job that grows in scope and complexity with age. Managing one disease is difficult, but managing two or three or more is a full-time job. Multiple doctors appointments, maintaining a diet, adhering to 5-plus medication regimens, managing symptoms, as well as the administration of communications between clinicians and insurers, grows to fill the time and patience available.

An Emerging Care Gap

Older adults are the CEOs of their own longevity. However, as frailty and capacity decline, they often rely on others. Who do we turn to? The state-of-the-art aging "technology" is a spouse, a partner or an oldest adult daughter. She, and it is most often "she," becomes the coordination and execution point for ensuring that the house is maintained and clean; food is prepared and eaten; trips are planned and driven; and, that health needs and administration are met. According to the Gallup-Healthways Wellbeing Index, nearly one-in-five American families provide 20-plus hours a week of caregiving to support the needs of an older loved one.

Fast forward. This is not your parent's old age. Boomers are turning 64, one every seven seconds. They had fewer children; are more likely to be divorced; are leading the fastest growing households in America — "households of one"; and, so far, most are aging-in-place in suburbs and rural areas where delivery of services is often problematic. What happens when the caregiver is distant or aging is a "home alone" experience?

Public agencies, such as Area Agencies on Aging, Visiting Nurses, hospitals, faith-based organizations and countless volunteer organizations provide a network of support to meet the most basic of needs. However, they are often overwhelmed and under-resourced. Short on budget, people, logistics and, sometimes, specialized expertise, these organizations vary widely in their capacity to deliver the services demanded by a population of older adults surging both in numbers and expectations.

Investing in Comprehensive, Collaborative and Connected Aging Services

The creative use of information communications technology (or ICT) can greatly improve the access to, and organization of, current aging services. ICT includes Web-based applications, social media, mobile communications (e.g., smart phones), and network and cloud computing. These are technologies that efficient consumer-facing organizations invest in to understand, respond and sometimes excite and delight their customer. Applied correctly, ICT can create new partnerships and provide intelligent connectivity between things and people forming a platform of care for older adults.

Businesses should develop and policymakers should invest in the deployment of applications and systems that advance three principles: comprehensive access, collaborative delivery and connected visibility.

Comprehensive Access— You are well and independent, until you are not. Few people plan, let alone can envision, the day they will need support with everyday activities. Consequently, the search for aging services is often after an event, such as a fall, or after a holiday meal when family members "discover" that a parent is not well.

Web-based technologies offer the potential to engage an older adult or caregiver in comprehensively thinking about what is needed now and is likely be needed soon. An automated geriatric care manager that can be consulted when many caregivers research their options — at a lunch break or late in the evening — may provide both the information and the connection to service providers.

Europe is investing in a variety of e-government initiatives to support aging. These include easy-to-use kiosks in post offices to access pension services as well as mobile phone applications to provide visibility of available transportation options on-demand. The United Kingdom's National Health Service even sponsors a social media application that collects and shares patient opinions at various facilities (e.g., wait times, parking, medical procedures).

Perhaps most helpful to older adults and caregivers alike is the potential to have one turnkey access point making eldercare simple. Partnerships between retailers and aging services providers may improve user awareness and access.

CVS, Target and others have already invested in retail clinics, providing easy and convenient access to medical services. Best Buy is focusing more on health and wellness. Could information communications technology be used to connect aging services with a retail face, simplicity and scale?

> **Perhaps most helpful to older adults and caregivers alike is the potential to have one turnkey access point making eldercare simple. Partnerships between retailers and aging services providers may improve user awareness and access.**

Collaborative Delivery — Aging is too big for government or business alone. Collaborative innovation will be required between public agencies and private firms to develop services and then deliver them. Public agencies today, such as the nation's more than

300 Area Agencies on Aging, have a vast and intimate knowledge of aging. However, their regional fragmentation and varied access to expertise and resources makes service delivery uneven. Private firms have technology and know how to scale service and product delivery, but have little knowledge about aging. Using technology to link public and private providers may produce better, more efficient services and open new markets.

Retailers such as Radio Shack and Walmart are within a few short miles of nearly 90 percent of the American population. Moreover, they have a finely tuned supply chain that makes it possible to source and deliver products efficiently and in real time. How might these supply chain efficiencies in retail be partnered with aging services? For example, could partnerships with food retailers, enabled by Web applications easily accessed by older adults, families or aging services providers, manage both customized nutritional needs and ensure timely, trusted delivery?

Home health services are another opportunity for collaborative innovation between retailers, pharmaceutical companies, Visiting Nurse associations and hospitals. A nascent example of things to come is Walgreens Health Initiatives, from the nation's largest pharmacy chain. WHI offers pharmacy benefits as well as home healthcare. These include infusion services, respiratory therapy and home medical equipment. In addition to clinical support, they work directly with insurers to manage coverage and administrative issues.

Connected Visibility—Information technology's basic value proposition is connectivity and communication. The jobs of aging and caregiving are often trying to connect and facilitate communication between providers, family members, payers, etc. Common platforms, such as a Web browser on the home computer, may provide a means for older adults to manage the services they are receiving. Banks have already developed relatively user-friendly and secure online systems for finance. Could these systems and retail banks provide a management tool for aging services? The same application on a workplace computer or a family caregiver's mobile phone may provide both efficient administration, as well as stress relief knowing that transportation, health or some other vital service has been delivered to an elderly parent.

Communications between providers is often lacking. For example, at times, the management of one or more chronic diseases can be easy, compared to ensuring that medical specialist "A" has spoken to specialist "B," "C," the pharmacist and the patient's primary care physician. Developing ubiquitous secure online tools that engage the clinicians *and* the patient or caregiver in collaborative decision making is likely to increase compliance as well as better outcomes.

Targeting Government and Business Investment

The growing demands of an aging population are a call to innovate. Targeted investment in information communications technology, as well as collaborative innovation by both government and business, will address the needs of older adults and their families. Done correctly, services will produce better outcomes and cost efficiencies, and stimulate new markets. Below are some guidelines on how to invest:

- **Stimulate collaborative innovation.** Invest in technologies and demonstrations that foster public-private partnerships. Partnerships should be based upon improved outcomes, as well as efficiencies and a sustainable economic business model.
- **Leverage "big" systems.** Wireless providers, cable companies, utilities, financial services and large retailers provide nearly

universal access to everyone. They are conduits into the homes and lives of older adults and caregivers. Investing in systems and services that leverage these "infrastructure" companies guarantees access, scalability and superior processes.

- **Touch the user not just the provider**. Systems that improve the "efficiency" of cost of service delivery alone may eventually benefit the public in the aggregate, but we age one at a time. Investments in systems and services that directly touch older adults are likely to produce better outcomes and are politically and economically sustainable.

- **Connect and distribute expertise**. Cisco's telemedicine demonstrations in California and elsewhere are good examples of bringing expertise to the user or patient. Additional investment should be made in using information communications technology to connect providers with each other and with lifelong education on best practices and technology in the full range of aging services (e.g., transportation, home modification, etc.).

WHO WILL BE IMAGINATIVE AND FLEXIBLE?

William L. (Larry) Minnix, Jr.

T here is a continuing evolution of aging services within the community of nonprofit providers. Many have histories dating back to the founding of our country. A major mission bulge was created 125-150 years ago precipitated by the social problems produced by the Civil War. That is when many of our members were founded. Philanthropy was the key economic engine.

Another major mission bulge took place with the advent of Great Society programs like Medicare and Medicaid. These bulges were driven, in part, by business opportunities imbedded in government coverage of care. While demographic need has grown in numbers and complexity, many current provider services have drifted to become product-reimbursement driven, instead of consumer need, mission driven — a paradigm ripe for change. This dynamic always occurs in transformation. It is easy to fall in love with our products and not recognize the ever-changing needs of the public.

So, the widows, orphans and veterans homes from the 1860s evolved into the rest homes of the pre-World War II era to the hospitals,

William L. (Larry) Minnix, Jr. is president and CEO of the American Association of Homes and Services for the Aging (AAHSA), a position he has held since 2001. Under his leadership at AAHSA, he has implemented major transformational initiatives around quality, talent, financing of aging services, technology and leadership initiatives including Leadership AAHSA. Minnix's career in aging services began in 1972 at what is now the Wesley Woods Center of Emory University, where he served for 28 years. Minnix has received numerous national awards, including being named to the *NonProfit Times'* 2008 "Power and Influence Top 50" list in 2008 and 2009.

nursing homes, health centers, rehab centers and retirement centers of the past two generations.

Language has changed to reflect public perception. Consumers of providers' services a century ago might have been called *inmates* or *incurables*. The people that governed and managed these services might have been labeled *boards of lady managers* or *superintendants*. The Medicare and Medicaid reimbursement era programs referred to consumers as patients, diagnostic labels or room numbers. Somewhere in this ever-changing language reflecting perception, terms like *elders*, *seniors*, *senior citizens* and *residents* emerged. Even *sweetie* and *honey* could be heard up and down nursing home corridors. *Residents* became a regulation-mandated term to replace *patients* in nursing homes.

The term *retirement* came into its own post-World War II as well. An arbitrary date was set for older people to quit work and get government money. Social science gurus of that day talked of disengagement theory where elders naturally withdrew from life's mainstream into institutions, or the quaint rocking chair. Also, retirement communities for those who can pay their own way emerged.

A common programmatic philosophy has been fairly pervasive through the first 200 years of services, regardless of setting or era. Common programs can be divided into two categories: *medical model care*—where it is assumed the inmates or patients are sick and the institution must treat them as such; and *entertainment service*—where it is assumed it is the job of staff to keep people busy with activities like bingo or shuffleboard. Paternalism has been alive and well in our field for some time.

Quality of service began to be defined and measured intensely a generation ago, when nursing home care was *outed* as inadequate.

Thousands of pages of regulations later, we now have quality defined by adherence to rules and routines often based on outdated clinical or management science — or no science at all. Years of government studies have yet to produce quality, as the consumer would define it.

The culture movement in nursing homes during the past 25 years has begun to mitigate against the institutional concepts so well ensconced. Putting "home" back in the nursing home, if it was ever there to begin with, is a major objective of these culture efforts. A new use of capital has begun to follow with the construction of smaller, more intimate home-style settings, not unlike some of the homes a century ago. Reconstruction of the large monolithic nursing home is fading rapidly. The culture movement has reminded us in the professional field of aging services about the humanity of the people we serve: their individuality, hopes, dreams, and interests new and old, regardless of impairments. AAHSA's members developed the culture movement, which began over a century ago, and now lead it ... again.

The culture movement has reminded us in the professional field of aging services about the humanity of the people we serve: their individuality, hopes, dreams, and interests new and old, regardless of impairments.

The era now, all too influenced by product-oriented, paternalistic, regulated dynamics is coming to an end. The new era will be consumer focused and directed, with tailored and flexible services that consider the individual within the context of family as they cope with chronic conditions that require support. We know that, quietly, the vast majority of services are delivered in the home setting by friends and family. These services are practical, unregulated and improvised according to family know-how and available resources. And they are augmented with newly emerging, often black-market support on a cash basis to keep older people with impairments and limitations stable within the context of families that work and go to school. Yes, children are caregivers and companions, too.

Not surprisingly, AAHSA founders prophesized in the early 1960s that our members are a basic social resource for the aged and their families; that the elderly will have economic power to choose lifestyles in later years; that most of us will want to live in independent settings as we age; that we will be driven by the search for privacy and yearning for the familiar; that great attention must be paid to mental illness and the flow from hospital to home; and that, ultimately, elderly people and their families will continually *seek opportunities for constructive living in our advanced years.*

That historic AAHSA report, written by Dr. Robert Morris of Brandeis, asked the fundamental question for providers then — and it applies now: Can we be sufficiently flexible and imaginative to develop requisite programs and services?

An old era, along with the age of inmates and incurables, is dying; and the age of retirement and disengagement is waning. The age of satisfaction, fulfillment and hope is emerging. What products and services will support those needs and wants? Imaginative and flexible providers will discover the answer. The rest will either follow or fade.

The nonprofit sector of AAHSA members — many of the same ones who pioneered the widows and old men's homes over a century ago — will lead the transformation to the next era. Society is counting on them to do so. 🕸

INNOVATING (FOR) GLOBAL AGING

————— Eric Dishman —————

t is the smell of my grandmother's farmhouse — especially the chicken and dumplings — that stays with me, even after I, sadly, can't quite hear the precise sound of her voice anymore. Going to her farm home was a welcome refuge, a place of warmth and love for me. Toward the end of her life, well into her 80s, her body failed — though never her mind — and my family couldn't care for her day-to-day needs without the help of a nursing home. I remember *those* smells, too, as the antiseptic and ammonia battled beneath a veneer of overpowering "air freshener" that was, ostensibly, pine-scented. These years later, I still wonder what would it have taken for grandma to have lived out her life in the home that we — and especially *she* — so loved?

Those memories have guided my career for two decades of exploring technologies that might give people more choice about where and how they live their "later years," even as age-related illnesses and infirmities take their toll. But a few caveats

Eric Dishman, a social scientist by training, is global director of health innovation and policy at Intel Corporation. He is responsible for driving research, new product innovation, strategic planning, and policy and standards activities in healthcare. In 2007, Dishman was named an Intel Fellow, one of only 46 Intel executives awarded this designation in recognition of industry leadership in science, technology and innovation. He is widely recognized as a global leader in driving healthcare reform through home and community-based technologies, focusing in particular in enabling seniors to live independently. He was named by the *Wall Street Journal* as one of "12 People Who Are Changing Your Retirement." Dishman also co-founded and serves as senior fellow for the Center for Aging Services Technologies (CAST), a nonprofit advocacy organization based in Washington, D.C.

are necessary before I talk more about technology. First, nursing homes — and the wider array of senior housing options that exist today than when my grandmother was alive — can be amazing (and often the best) places for many people. Second, technology is just a tool and something that we shouldn't celebrate as a magical cure-all. Third, the innovative care models and social contracts that technology can enable are what should excite us the most.

Just as global warming has sparked new government investments and industries to meet those enormous challenges, so, too, must global aging catalyze new technologies, industries and jobs that address this disruptive demography.

Our swiftly aging population needs to find answers to the aging-in-place challenge. Just as global warming has sparked new government investments and industries to meet those enormous challenges, so, too, must *global aging* catalyze new technologies, industries and jobs that address this disruptive demography. We must rev-up the innovation engine to help Boomers-as-seniors live long, healthy, productive lives in their homes and communities with social support systems in which we all enlist.

For the past decade, Intel Corporation and our university collaborators have been inventing and testing these kinds of innovations. Through ethnographic fieldwork of more than 1,000 households in 20 countries and dozens of research pilots in hundreds of homes, Intel has strived to discover what works, what breaks, what is useful, and what is compelling to seniors, families and their care networks. Our most successful innovations have consistently enabled *Choice, Connection* and *Compassion.*

Choice

How can we give older people and their families more choice about where they live, even as they face multiple chronic conditions, mobility challenges, struggles doing daily activities, or memory problems? What can help the majority of seniors who would prefer to age-in-place from the comfort and safety of their own homes? Home sensor networks — very similar to the technologies already installed for home security systems — combined with personal computers and software offer great promise. The first prototype built at Intel was the "tea making assistant" that used simple wireless sensors to remind someone with memory loss that they weren't getting enough to eat or drink. The biggest challenge for the system was providing *timely*, meaningful prompts — short videos from the family triggered on the den or kitchen television — to help the person remember the steps for daily tasks like making tea or fixing a bowl of cereal.

Today, Intel is experimenting with "magic carpet" sensors in the floor, as well as small wearable sensors the size of a matchbox, that might be used to detect subtle changes in movement around the house that are predictive of someone being at risk for a fall. Intel also has conducted research to try to detect the onset of cognitive decline by utilizing software that evaluates performance playing games on the PC — such as solitaire — to see if someone is taking longer to make a move, is losing more games than they used to, or is no longer playing as frequently. Similar sensors and software have been used to prompt people to take just the right pill at just the right time through reminders on the phone, TV, watch, cell phone, PC or an audio prompter. If these kinds of innovation succeed, it is possible that in a generation or two, no one will even understand the concept of a "nursing home," except in history books.

Connection

How can we give older people tools to keep them socially connected and engaged; and what connections can we make among seniors, their families, and professional care or service providers? Much of Intel's research has focused on fostering social connection. Early on, a concept was tested in the homes of people suffering with early Alzheimer's to help them answer the phone with confidence (one participant called it "Caller I.D. on Steroids") through a simple screen next to their landline that showed the picture, relationship and history of conversations with the person making the incoming call. Intel also built prototypes that allowed seniors to manage their chronic conditions from their own homes in an attempt to avoid the hassles, costs and risks of a hospital or clinic visit while staying closely connected to their nurse or doctor. They could do a video "virtual visit," receive reminders/prompts to collect their vital signs, and review customized educational content to self-manage their diabetes, hypertension or cardiovascular disease.

More recently, Intel tested prototypes that allow seniors to schedule "audio chat" sessions — like the party lines of yesteryear — to teach a class, just hang out, or share photos and stories with either friends or strangers online. Technologies have helped people watch television "together" across thousands of miles. Seniors on a long-term care campus — even veterans from the same World War II unit — have been enabled to use online tools to discover old friends who were living a half block away. These innovations are about enabling new kinds of social relationships, in person and remotely, with familiars and with strangers. Perhaps in a generation or two, the walls and distances between seniors and their care networks will come down, and the isolation and depression that is so commonplace today among older people will become an anachronism.

Compassion

How can we enable a new "care force" of family members, neighbors and volunteers to help with the care of our aging population? One answer Intel prototyped is a PC "dashboard" that a neighbor can use to virtually "check in" on a frail friend, while the spouse of that friend gets a few hours of much-needed respite. Similar sensing technologies were used to build a "presence lamp" that was given to caregivers in a social support group for families dealing with Alzheimer's. The lamp in one caregiver's house would turn on when one of their friends was up and awake, and vice versa. Thus, when awakened for hours by a loved one suffering from advanced Alzheimer's, the caregiver's lamp would turn on, showing them that one of their fellow caregivers also happened to be awake and was available for a phone call and some moral support — even at 3:30 in the morning.

Intel also repurposed off-the-shelf technologies to help neighbors help one another. A GPS system was installed in the cars of seniors who still drove. Then, their typical routes were shared with other seniors in the village who could no longer drive. Soon, a "virtual ride board" emerged where seniors were driving seniors to hair appointments, grocery stores and the library — giving the driver a sense of purpose, the rider a chance to leave their home, and both a new bond that had never been there before. In a generation or two, these kinds of innovations could lead to a very different notion of what a "neighborhood" is or how we can volunteer to help. And perhaps these tools will make it possible, even routine, for friends and family members to work part-time in the care of their loved ones without having to give up their whole jobs, salaries and own health to provide 24/7 informal care.

Innovation and the Marketplace

So, after 10 years of study by Intel and many others, why are these innovations still stuck primarily in the laboratory as explorations, experiments and prototypes? While there are some great early products out there that begin to achieve the vision of independent living — that provide some *Choice, Connection* and *Compassion* — this "marketplace" is almost non-existent. The products so far are primarily "point products" to solve specific problems. There really aren't yet holistic systems and services that can be purchased to, for example, enable my grandmother to have lived safely in her own home for those final years.

Our society's inherent ageism — especially when it comes to technology and innovation — is a big part of the problem. We focus, almost obsessively, on youth culture and markets. We have too often pathologized aging — treating it as a disease to be cured with a pill — while searching for the next medical miracle that achieves greater longevity as the sole measure of all progress. Perhaps science fiction offers a way to move these products from fantasy to reality. I am reminded of "Star Trek" and Mr. Spock's frequent mantra to "live long and prosper." As a society, we've done amazing things with modern medical technologies to enable "live long." Now let's focus together on "prosper." We can create economic prosperity by investing in innovative care models and independent living technologies that promote the prosperity of everyday life for our aging population. This is perhaps our generation's *space race* — our moon landing — to enable *choice, connection* and *compassion* for seniors ... in ways we never previously imagined.

AFFIRMATIVE AGING AT EVERY AGE

———— Donna M. Butts ————

W hen in doubt, consult a doctor. In this case, Dr. Seuss, who cautioned us about the dreaded waiting places we encounter in life when he wrote *Oh the Places You'll Go!* Still, we stumble when it comes to creating new age phases.

Take adolescence for example, it didn't exist until the beginning of the 20th century when child laborers were no longer in keen demand. We gave young people the gift of a new time in life without definition or responsibility. Adolescence became a "waiting place," complete with the message "you're too young to contribute and waiting to be." As the time spent in older age grows longer and healthier, this new stage is in danger of becoming another "waiting place" where people go who are "too old to contribute and waiting to die." This tendency to ignore and not engage the bookend generations — our young and old — put our country at risk of losing new ideas and huge amounts of energy at a time when these resources are sorely needed. Breaking down age silos and taking an intergenerational approach to program and policy development will strengthen our neighborhoods, communities and families.

Donna M. Butts has served as executive director of Generations United (www.gu.org) since 1997. Prior to joining GU, Butts served as executive director of the National Organization of Adolescent Pregnancy, Parenting and Prevention. Her more than 30 years of experience working with nonprofit youth development organizations at local, national and international levels includes holding leadership positions with the YWCA, Covenant House and the National 4-H Council.

Why encourage intergenerational approaches now? It's time to wake up and smell the demographics. The world is aging and youth are engaging. Life expectancy and healthier, older age are on the rise. By the year 2030, the number of people over the age of 65 is expected to double to 70 million or one in every five people. The fastest growing population will be those 85 and older. Most Boomers report they do not intend to retire in any traditional manner. They see retirement as a time to write another chapter, not close the book. Many, 70 percent, say they want to try new things and 81 percent report they want to learn new things. Rather than move to the adult communities, most say they want to continue to live in the age-integrated towns in which they have worked and played. Intergenerational programs offer older adults a venue to do what many do well: help grow the next generation.

Most Boomers report they do not intend to retire in any traditional manner.

At the same time, the other bookend generation, our children and youth, continue to be marginalized despite the fact that volunteering among high school students has reached the highest level in 50 years. Young people today are more likely to be engaged in one-to-one service on behalf of their communities than their predecessors. The Independent Sector reports that 59.3 percent of teens between the ages of 12 and 17 volunteer, and 70 percent of teens report participating in activities to improve their communities. Rather than viewing young people as problems to be solved, more opportunities are being created for them to exercise and demonstrate their leadership abilities. Youth involved in volunteer programs continue to give their time, contribute money to charitable causes and serve in leadership positions at higher rates than the general population. Indeed, two-thirds of today's adult volunteers report they started volunteering when they were young.

Intergenerational programs provide an extra benefit as children and youth learn that older adults are people too and aging doesn't have to be scary. Still, intergenerational programs are more likely to be considered nice — more of a side dish — than life-saving or invaluable to community building. We need to seize the opportunity the current economic landscape provides and, once and for all, eliminate artificial age segregation and encourage the proliferation of intergenerational practices and public policies. Two examples are ripe for attention.

First, intergenerational shared sites are gaining traction in communities around the country. Local governments are learning their funds go further when they build multigenerational centers rather than separate senior centers, teen centers, child care centers and recreation centers. Others have learned about the psychological and health value of combining adult day care with child care or after school programs with nursing homes. "Gen Joints" such as these demonstrate that we are stronger together and that resources are better used when they connect generations rather than separate them. We can save dollars while making sense.

Second, Social Security continues to be debated in this country. What's missing is the understanding that it is a family program and not a retirement program. By encouraging the transfer of resources from one generation of workers to the next, Social Security gives expression to the value of community. However, the intergenerational importance of Social Security is usually left out of the dialogue. Those interested in reducing the federal government or who erroneously believe they can reallocate federal dollars use language like "leaving a legacy" or "we can't unfairly burden the next generation" and hide behind grandchildren. They ignore the fact that that Social Security is an intergenerational social insurance program. It embodies the social compact that is so fundamental to civil society and recognizes that across the life course everyone will give and receive care at various times. While past debates have focused on retirement income for older adults, in fact one-third of Social Security recipients are under the age of 65, including those receiving survivor and disability benefits. Social Security alone lifts more than 1 million children out of poverty each year, second only to the Earned Income Tax Credit, and is one of the primary financial supports for children being raised by grandparents. Still, many in the children and youth field are unaware of the important role the program plays in the lives of these populations. We need to shine light on the neglected elements of the program; and, rather than stumble over a limited pie frame, focus on adequacy and strengthening Social Security for all generations and all families.

Intergenerational approaches can be a source of social cohesion. Collaboration across the generations makes the whole larger than the sum of the parts in advocacy as well as programs. Together the bookend generations hold together a civil society that builds strong neighborhoods, strong families and a strong future.

In 1986, David Liederman, then head of the Child Welfare League of America, and Jack Ossofsky, then head of the National Council on Aging, formed Generations United, based on the belief that competition between the generations was counterintuitive. Only united could the generations thrive. At the news conference announcing the new organization, Ossofsky said, "We believe that the time is long past when advocates for children, families and the elderly can afford separate agendas. We foresee a new and brighter America when organizations representing different age groups can join forces to strengthen our communities." Ossofsky later said, "We formed Generations United to argue for a caring society." Over 20 years ago, they knew we are stronger together. ▣

THE FUTURE IS IN AGRITOPIA, OR SWAMPSCOTT

John Martin and Matt Thornhill

One day, historians will look back upon the decade of the 2000s as the last gasp of the peculiar practice, dating back to Sun City in Arizona a half-century before, in which older citizens of the United States voluntarily segregated themselves from their families, their communities and the rest of society.

As anecdotal evidence, future historians could well point to the dismal opening in early 2009 of Fox Hill, a luxury condominium development for seniors in Bethesda, Maryland.

The $300 million project offers the usual amenities expected from an assisted living facility, plus luxuries. The condos spare no expense: They have nine-foot ceilings, gas fireplaces and crown molding. The resort-like complex, built next to a golf course, houses four restaurants, a salon and spa, a recording studio, an art studio, an indoor driving range and a wine cellar. Condos range in price from $557,000 to $1.8 million.

John Martin and Matt Thornhill run the Boomer Project (www.boomerproject.com), a marketing research and consulting firm specializing in helping marketers better understand today's older Boomer consumer. Their clients include Johnson & Johnson, AARP, Walmart, Lincoln Financial, American Healthcare Association, Home Instead Senior Care and dozens of other organizations. Thornhill has spoken at national conferences for the American Healthcare Association and the National Center for Assisting Living, and at the California Association of Healthcare Facilities annual conference. Martin has spoken at two Aging Services of California events and at state healthcare association conferences across the country. They are the co-authors of the award-winning book, *Boomer Consumer*.

From a business perspective, what sets Fox Hill apart is that it doesn't rent its units or charge nonrefundable entrance fees. It sells its condos to residents on the logic — which seemingly made sense two or three years ago — that its silver-haired customers would value the opportunity to participate in rising real estate prices. But, by late June 2009, only 54 of its 240 units had sold over the past six months.

Clearly, the crash in residential real estate prices and the collapse of investment portfolios has put a damper on Fox Hill sales. But future historians may conclude that the senior housing market of 2008/9 also had reached a sociological inflection point. The luxury that many retirees craved wasn't crown molding or high ceilings, but the simple comforts of their own home. The amenity they sought wasn't a wine cellar or a golf course, but sharing in the lives of their children and grandchildren.

Here at the Boomer Project, we foresee momentous changes coming to the older adult living industry. Boomers have reinvented nearly every institution they've touched in their long, strange journey through life, and we expect they will continue to do so as they grow older. Our market research surveys consistently show the same thing: By a large margin, most Boomers want to live in the same house, or at least the same community, as they do now. They feel younger than they are, and they want to interact with people younger than they are.

Proponents of intergenerational living believe that life is richer and more fulfilling when the generations remain interconnected. Attention tends to focus on the two groups that are most likely to be segregated by generation: children (in schools) and older adults (in assisted living communities).

"Age segregation robs a child of many meaningful, beneficial relationships," writes "Intentional Parents" blog author Sonya Shafer.

Increasingly, the same argument against age segregation applies to older adults, too.

From 1776 until 1960, when Sun City started selling homes, many American households contained multiple generations under one roof. The practice went out of style when the ideal of the nuclear family — mom, dad and children — became the ideal. But the atomization of the family unit into ever smaller households has reversed itself. Intergenerational families are becoming normal, if not yet the norm. According to the U.S. Census Bureau, 2.3 million older parents were living with adult children in 2000; by 2007, that number had jumped to 3.6 million — a 50 percent increase.

But the atomization of the family unit into ever smaller households has reversed itself. Intergenerational families are becoming normal, if not yet the norm.

While increased family togetherness could be seen as a sign of economic hardship — it saves on shelter/housing costs — most see intergenerational living as a positive. Indeed, a grassroots movement touting the virtues of intergenerational living is spreading across the country. Americans are rediscovering the benefits of inter-connectedness. For the most part, intergenerational projects are small, arising mostly from the nonprofit and educational sectors, although some real estate developers are catching on as well. Places like Swampscott and Agritopia point the way to the future.

Swampscott, a Massachusetts township, stumbled into an intergenerational project almost by accident. The senior center for the small town was located in an 1870s-era house that was busting at the seams. The tight quarters provided little room for educational or recreational activities. Blood-pressure testing took place in the lunch room.

Someone got the idea of attaching a new senior center to a proposed new high school. Students and older adults could share facilities like a gymnasium, fitness center, music suite, piano lab, aerobics studio, lecture halls, and arts and crafts studio. Fiscally and politically, the move made sense — voters approved a bond referendum to fund the joint project in 2005. As a bonus, it was hoped, the intergenerational contact would enrich the lives of both the younger and older generations.

And it has worked: Teens provided tutorials on computer skills, e-mail, programming cell phones and the use of digital cameras and VCR equipment. Twenty-five fifth graders adopted pen pals among the town's seniors. During Veterans Day remembrances, WWII and Korean War veterans participated in panel discussions.

We expect to see more of these combinations of "old with young" popping up all over ... but there is a much bigger market opportunity in conventional real estate development — building communities from scratch that are organized around intergenerational living. The problem is that most residential neighborhoods built today are aimed at specific demographic slices. Municipal codes mandate single-family dwellings for nuclear families. Homeowner covenants prohibit the construction of additional units for additional households. Granny flats, garage apartments, bungalows and other small dwellings for one or two people are literally zoned out of existence.

At least one developer is tackling the problem head on. The Johnston brothers of Gilbert, Arizona. are developing a farm-centered community they call "Agritopia." "We believe that it is important to focus on people rather than 'stuff,'" they explain on their website. "People are the most valuable result of creation, and meaningful relationships between people are to be fostered. A simpler life, devoting time to relationships, rather than acquiring and maintaining 'stuff' is a richer life."

At the Boomer Project, we think the Johnston brothers are plugged into the spirit of the times. Millions of Americans are reacting to the past two decades' debt-financed orgy of overconsumption by cutting spending, paying down debt and living with less "stuff." Simultaneously, we are witnessing the spread of the Green movement, which blames conspicuous consumption for everything from energy waste to pollution and global warming. We expect to see a broad movement away from living arrangements like Sunrise Living's Fox Hill, which emphasize material amenities, toward arrangements like Agritopia, which fosters relationships.

Sales have slowed at Agritopia, too, but the project is well-positioned to recover when the real estate market does. A unique feature of the development is zoning that allows nearly all home-owners to incorporate an "auxiliary unit" into a detached garage, and for many to build a stand-alone, 800-square-foot bungalow in the back of the lot. Say the Johnstons: "This means that the owner of the lot can live in the main residence and have a smaller unit for older parents, a college son or daughter, or even as a rental unit."

Agritopia's vision is in sync with broad social trends that are reshaping society — and, ultimately, the housing market. According to Home Instead Senior Care, 43 percent of all adult caregivers in the United States ages 35 to 62 reside with the parent or other older relative for whom they or someone else in their household provide care. As the population ages, more Americans will find themselves looking after older relatives — and/or relying upon them to help with their grandchildren. While some families are harmonious enough for everyone to all live in the same dwelling, many are not. Often, the best arrangement is to live nearby but separately. Bungalows and granny flats are the wave of the future, assuming zoning codes and homeowner covenants loosen up enough to allow them.

We expect society's focus to shift from the design of assisted living projects, where older adults are segregated from society, to the redesign and retrofitting of entire communities, where not only the housing stock but signage, streetscapes, transportation systems and services for older adults are made to accommodate their needs. Municipalities that make these changes will serve their older constituents far better than communities that assume that the future will look like the past, only more so.

In our home state of Virginia, the Boomer Project has been privileged to be involved with the Older Dominion Project (www. olderdominion.org), a consortium of governments, nonprofits and private companies that are planning for the *age wave*. We don't pretend to know yet what the new model for housing for older adults will look like, but at least we've started the conversation.

Based on what we've learned, we do venture this prediction: Intergenerational living is the wave of the future. Developers who figure out how to tap that dynamic will rule the market over the next two to three generations. ▣

MARKETING: AGE IS MORE THAN JUST A NUMBER

—————— Brent Bouchez ——————

s ageism at play in marketing and advertising in this country? The answer is a resounding *yes*.

Just look around: How many mainstream products do you see that advertise to an older group or even feature older people in their ads? None. Unless, of course, the appeal happens to be directed toward the aging, such as for Viagra or Crestor or Depends or any number of "You poor thing, here's something that can help" products. These ads do feature older consumers, though mostly in a pitiful light.

Cars, clothes, computers, cosmetics, consumer electronics, fast food, travel, insurance, cell phones, credit cards, banks, you name it; to look at the advertising and marketing for any of these categories, you would assume that the only people with money in their wallets are under 35 years old.

And in assuming that, you could not be more wrong.

About 75 percent of the wealth in America is in the wallets of people over age 50. This group earns $2.4 trillion annually, while the under-34 group earns $1 trillion. Consumers 50-plus have 2.5 times the discretionary spending power of any other consumer cohort and

Brent Bouchez is co-founder of the New York-based Agency Five-0, which develops messaging, content and creative campaigns to reach the age 50-plus consumer. His clients include BMW Automobiles, Nike, Bank of America, Nikon, *The New York Times*, MILK, Porsche Cars and Verizon, among many others. His professional career includes creative positions with Chiat/Day and Ketchum in Los Angeles; and Ammirati & Puris, M&C Saatchi and Bozell in New York.

they stand to inherit between $14 and $20 trillion dollars in the next 15 years, the largest generational inheritance in history and likely the largest that will ever be. According to McKinsey Consulting, consumers over age 50 buy 60 percent of all packaged goods, 56 percent of all new cars, 80 percent of leisure travel and in 2010 they will account for 50 percent of all consumer spending — period.

And yet, less than 10 percent of all marketing dollars are spent targeting the 50-plus consumer. Nationwide research shows that the majority of consumers over 50 feel that advertising either portrays them negatively or ignores them altogether.

So, given those kinds of numbers, I would say the case could certainly be made for ageism in marketing and advertising.

But the more I think about it, the more I think ageism is the wrong word.

Maybe a better word would be *stupidity*. It's stronger and more to the point. Honestly, if you are in the business of selling things and you ignore the largest, fastest growing, richest consumer segment on the face of the earth, it seems that you are simply stupid.

So, now that I've offended every chief marketing officer in the land, let me say that they may have come by this stupidity quite naturally and by no real fault of their own.

Today's advertising agencies are full of young, talented people whose job it is to create messages for a world of consumers who look, act and feel just like they do. In advertising parlance, reaching the 18-34-year-old demographic is called targeting the "sweet spot." Ninety percent of today's marketing dollars are spent trying to reach this group. Marketers lust after them and media companies do everything in their power to lure them to their websites, magazines, TV shows and radio stations.

This strategy made perfect sense in '70s, when 18-34-year-olds were smack in the middle of the Baby Boom. Back then, they were the sweet spot of the sweet spot, the "pig in the python," the largest group of consumers in history with the most money to spend. In the '70s and '80s and even some of the '90s, Boomers could make or break a brand. They could also make or break an advertising agency. Thanks in large part to the Baby Boom, Madison Avenue entered a gilded age. Agencies that knew how to reach the 18-34 demographic attracted the best clients and the most income. For the first time, advertising agencies were bought and sold for hundreds of millions of dollars and even traded on the stock exchange right next to their clients. Agency executives, many of them Boomers themselves, made previously unheard of fortunes. Chief marketing officers made their own, albeit smaller, fortunes and along the way, 18-34-year-olds — the "youth" demographic — became not just the sweet spot for marketing, they became the only spot for marketing.

Unfortunately, biology being what it is, 30 years later, the "pig" has moved to the other, older end of the "python." People 50-plus now generate 41 percent of all disposable income; and they spend $2.5 trillion a year and show no signs of slowing down. In fact, 90 percent of people 50-plus say they intend to work well into their 60s and beyond. This means they will also continue spending apace.

Now, if you are a chief financial officer and reading this, you're probably wondering why, if people over 50 spend two and a half times more than their 18-34 counterparts, is your marketing department and your advertising agency still fixated on the younger generation?

The answer: in their minds, youth equals success. Youth is what made Madison Avenue a publicly traded industry. *But times they are a changing.* And sadly, Madison Avenue continues to live by a set of rules written three decades ago, even though the present and the future, as the numbers above indicate, look very different.

What are those old rules?

From an AARP Top Ten List of misconceptions about consumers 50-plus: Older consumers don't spend money. They don't change brands. They don't try new things. They're not tech savvy. Older consumers aren't cool. They're hard to reach with advertising. And my particular favorite, they (we) won't live long enough for the marketing investment to pay off.

Not surprisingly, many of these misconceptions were quite true 30 years ago. Today however, as the AARP study goes on to point out and as the numbers above make abundantly clear, the world could not be more different.

Today's 50-plus consumers spend at a rate of 2.5 times that of younger consumers. They are actually more likely to switch brands than people in their 20s and 30s. They are happy to experiment and prove it by purchasing more hybrid automobiles than any other segment (remember, in the 70s, 80s and 90s, this group went from buying American cars to Japanese to German to Korean cars). The 50-plus crowd is online in greater absolute numbers than any other cohort and in fourth quarter 2007, they spent nearly three times the national average for holiday shopping online.

Reach the 50-plus with advertising? This is the group that turned the Superbowl into the *Commercial Bowl* and gave rise to the *USA Today* Superbowl commercial ratings that so many marketers can't wait to tout. And never mind the fact that the average television viewer today is 50 years old. When it comes to the cool factor, just consider the following: Madonna, Alec Baldwin, Oprah, Denzel Washington, Bono, Dolce & Gabana, Steve Jobs, Ellen, Muccia Prada, Bruce Willis, the Coen Brothers, Anna Wintour, David Letterman ... and you get the idea, are all over 50 years old.

As for my favorite misconception, the one about me not being worth the investment because I'm going to be checking out soon: The average life expectancy for an American male today is somewhere around 79 years old, which gives me another 27 years of shopping to do. Hardly a short time in a world where the average CMO's tenure is around 24 months.

When presented with all of the above — the numbers that paint a picture of opportunity unlike any we have ever seen from one consumer category; and the data that shows this to not be a trend but a new reality — I suppose I can't suggest that ageism or even stupidity is at fault for marketers not taking advantage of the situation. It's actually something much less evil, but in marketing, much more unforgivable: ignorance.

BEHAVIORAL

ELDERTOPIA

―――――― William H. Thomas, M.D. ――――――

O ur longevity is an ancient thing. It came into being long before the beginning of recorded history and it is intrinsic to the experience of being human. Longevity is also a matter of urgent contemporary concern. We live in world where influential voices claim that humanity's flourishing longevity is actually a disaster in the making. A string of aging-related economic and cultural catastrophes are forecast to descend upon us all.

I do not tremble before the "Senior Tsunami." It is much more fun (and useful) to celebrate the fact that we are entering into history's most elder-rich era. From the beginning, human elderhood has been protected, sustained and nurtured because it serves vital human interests. Old age exists today only because thousands of generations of our ancestors found it to be useful. Our unique pattern of longevity — we are the only creature capable of living so far beyond the period of reproductive maturity — now lies at the core of our humanity. Alone among all other creatures, we benefit from a stage of life that extends beyond adulthood. For millennia, our ancestors have

William H. Thomas, M.D. is the grandson of Olive, Durwood, Vivian and William. He is also a farmer, novelist, teamster, musician and geriatrician. An innovator in the aging field, he is the founder of the Eden Alternative and the Green House Project; and author of numerous books including *What Are Old People For? How Elders Will Save the World*. He currently serves a professor of the practice of aging studies at the University of Maryland's Erickson School. His approach to the new culture of aging can be followed on his blog at www.changingaging.org.

understood elderhood to be as distinct from adulthood as adulthood is from childhood.

Life in a modern industrial society makes it difficult to embrace, or even imagine, our own elderhood. We live under the sway of a ravenous worldwide addiction to the virtues of adulthood, which, not coincidentally, also reinforces the idea of old age as tired, worn and uniformly undesirable. Old people as individuals may be laudable, but as a group they have been redefined as useless appendages to human society.

Advocates for the aged work to promote the vision of a society wherein the aged are elevated to a status equal to that accorded to the young, forgetting that the strength of elderhood lies in how radically different from adulthood it is. This dismissal of elderhood is an epic error on par with a rejection of fire-making and the wheel.

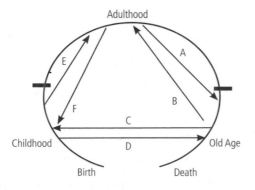

This figure depicts the intergenerational transmission of culture and assistance.

A. Support provided to elders by adults

B. Assistance elders give to adults

C. Gentling and acculturation of children by elders

D. Assistance and affection given to elders by children

E. Participation in work of adults by children

F.   Food, shelter, clothing and affection provided to children by adults

The diagram offers a schematic representation of the engine that has powered human cultural advancement for tens of thousands of years. It has shaped us, served us, blunted our worst tendencies and magnified our best. Given the terrible might of modern industrial society, it would seem that we need this engine more than ever before. Instead, we are witness to the rise of an "anti-aging" movement — which continues to claim, despite all evidence to the contrary, that technology will soon make old age a thing of the past. Deep down, most people understand that aging is an inevitable part of life. What confounds us is the question, "What are old people for?"

Former Colorado Governor Richard Lamm adopted the classic "aging is a disaster" (for the young) perspective in his essay, "The Moral Imperative of Limiting Elderly Entitlements." He writes, "One of the great challenges in America's future is to retire the Baby Boomers without bankrupting the country or unduly burdening future generations... Age could well be as divisive in the next forty years."

What is missing here is an accounting of what elderhood contributes *to* society. This side of the ledger is regularly ignored by those who believe an Iron Curtain exists between the wealth and vigor of adults and the ruinous burden that age imposes on the young. Lamm goes on to declare, "We are a compassionate society and we can afford a lot, but we cannot afford everything. No publicly financed health system can ignore the law of diminishing returns ... It is necessary to find, among the myriad of things that we can do, what practically in a budget we ought to do."

Old people become expensive accessories and, while we may be a "compassionate society," there is a limit to what *we* can do for *them*. What we need is a radical interpretation of longevity that properly values elders (and their needs) as being essential to our collective pursuit of happiness and well-being. It should not come as a surprise that our language lacks a word that describes the interdependence that joins young and old. The wisdom of living in a multigenerational social structure is ancient, undeniable and deserving of a word of its own. I like "Eldertopia."

> **Eldertopia** / ell-der-TOE-pee-uh / *noun* —A community that improves the quality of life for people of all ages by strengthening and improving the means by which (1) the community protects, sustains, and nurtures its elders, and (2) the elders contribute to the well-being and foresight of the community. An Eldertopia that is blessed with a large number of older people is acknowledged to be "elder-rich" and uses this richness to the advantage of all.

Our longevity exists, has meaning and creates value because it provides human beings with a mechanism for improving the lives of people of all ages. Far from being society's expensive leftovers, elders and the elderhood they inhabit are crucial to the functioning of healthy human societies. We tabulate the money spent serving the elderly to the penny but fail to appreciate the vital contributions that our longevity makes to society as a whole. We need a new and much more accurate system of accounting.

The pursuit of Eldertopia can lead us with a better understanding of how longevity completes us. For a start, it can illuminate the complex and easily overlooked intergenerational transfers that are essential to people of all ages. The "greedy geezer" stereotype can be seen as the inevitable product of a society that measures only the assistance the young grant to the old. Giving proper due to the contributions elders make to the young undermines anti-old age prejudice. Understood in their proper context, elders and elderhood can be seen as the best investment human beings have ever made.

So, what are old people for? They are the glue that binds us together as human beings. We need elders because we need families, congregations, neighborhoods and communities. We need Eldertopia because old age is a precious gift, one honed over the centuries. It exists to connect us with our past, and to our future. ◉

LISTEN, LEARN AND LIVE TO BE 100

Neenah Ellis

I am not a doctor, a professor or a politician. I'm a journalist. I observe and describe. And after many, many hours of visiting centenarians in their own homes, I have an opinion about how to improve the lives of seniors in this country.

At the turn of this century, I interviewed more than 25 centenarians, people 100 years old or older, for a series on National Public Radio called "One Hundred Years of Stories." I learned a lot about the difficulties of being very old in this country, but most importantly I learned the value of deep listening.

When you are 100 years old, your life expectancy is 18 months and that fact brought some urgency to our task. With my tape recorder running, I sat on ancient living room couches all over the country and listened to centenarians tell me their life stories. They talked for hours and hours: three, four, five hours at a stretch; sometimes for two or three days in a row.

Many of them couldn't see or hear well, so I sat very close. "Sit right there so I can see your face," said Helen Boardman, age 102. Some of the women wanted to hold my hand.

"Are you sure you want all this?" they would ask. And when I said *yes*, they talked like there was no tomorrow. I heard stories about life

Neenah Ellis is a radio documentary producer, the author of *The New York Times* bestseller *If I Live to be 100: Lessons from the Centenarians* and the general manager of public radio station WYSO in Yellow Springs, Ohio. She is formerly a producer for NPR's "All Things Considered."

before electricity, about courting by horse-drawn sleigh in Vermont, about lynchings in the South, about Civil War veterans marching in Brooklyn on the fourth of July, about tent revivals during the Great Depression. I think they thought it was their last chance to get their stories told, to go on the record. They all took it very seriously.

During the first few interviews I asked a lot of questions, historical ones, mostly. Most of the centenarians had lived in three centuries, after all, and had seen the world change drastically around them, but many of them weren't all that interested in talking about the past.

"I don't think about the past," said Abraham Goldstein. "The past is gone." Abe was still teaching law in New York, focused very much on the future. I took a cue from Abe, threw out my list of questions and tried instead to find the uniqueness of each life.

Like him, many wanted to talk about their work. For others, family stories came out. A few wanted to talk about the Lord. I learned to listen without judging and without interrupting because the less I talked, the deeper they went, the richer the details. I tried to learn to nod and just let them keep going.

They told me stories that their own families hadn't heard. One lady confessed that she had never loved her husband, but had married him because he was "a good kisser." One told me the exact day he got false teeth. "Gee," he said, "I'm really telling you everything, aren't I?" He went on to describe how, one night, he heard the ghost of his late wife enter his bedroom.

I did not ask the centenarians the one question that everyone else seems to ask first: What's your secret ... how did you get to be so old?

Now, it's important to know here that there are more than 70,000 centenarians in the United States and a third of them are healthy and active. Many of them have never had a major illness. That's a lot of healthy, active centenarians. Hundreds in every state.

And the truth is, they have no idea how they got to be so old and so healthy. None whatsoever. Ask the question about "their secret" and you could get an answer like: "moon pies and Coca-Cola."

So instead I asked questions such as: What is it like to *be* 100 years old? How do you manage to stay in your own home? How do you not get isolated when you can't drive or socialize? What is it like to have outlived everyone you grew up with, your spouse, your children? What do you dream about?

I was looking for practical information about how to live at an advanced age and I got advice, lots of it. "Keep moving." "Don't sit home alone." "Do something with yourself."

Many of them had similar personalities. They were outgoing. They didn't feel sorry for themselves and didn't have trouble asking for what they needed. They were direct. And, significantly, I think, they had plans for the future. They were not sad and depressed and counting their days. They had something in their lives much bigger than themselves.

I mentioned Abe Goldstein, who was still teaching law. Harry Shapiro, also in New York, was a painter and went to his studio every day, determined to tell stories through his art. Margaret Rawson was an international authority on dyslexia and kept up with the scientific literature, even though she was nearly blind. Another fellow, Roy Larkin Stamper, a preacher from Oklahoma, desperate to save souls while he still could, got married to a woman who heard my story about him on the radio. He was 103.

After two years of meeting centenarians and hundreds of hours of interviews, here is what I concluded. It sounds simple but it is not.

Most of my centenarians knew the therapeutic effect of a good long conversation. They wanted to touch another person, they were ready and eager to talk, but they had trouble finding someone who would take the time to listen.

Did they talk with me so long because I was making a documentary and they wanted publicity? I don't think so. *After* we had talked for hours, I would turn my tape recorder off and as I packed up my gear they would ask, "Where are you from again?" or "Which newspaper do you write for?" They didn't care that I was making a documentary about them. They needed to talk, to make sense of their long years on earth, to understand what it means to live so long.

The elderly are infantilized, trivialized by the people who have the greatest opportunity to listen. It's no wonder seniors get grouchy and bitter.

Too many times I have visited with seniors in the presence of a healthcare worker and I inevitably heard lots of lighthearted joking in loud voices along the lines of "Aren't you looking beautiful today? Did you get your hair done?" Or, "You are a real ladykiller in that blue shirt!"

I can't stand to hear that condescending tone of voice. When you have to raise your voice — because the elderly are often hard of hearing — it's easy to do. The elderly are infantilized, trivialized by the people who have the greatest opportunity to listen. It's no wonder seniors get grouchy and bitter.

There is a book I want to mention, titled *A General Theory of Love*, which explains that (and this is a highly abbreviated summary) as mammals, we have a brain structure called the limbic region, which allows us to feel the emotional states of other mammals. If we can be quiet long enough, and just sit with someone and read their body language, we can begin to feel the emotions they are feeling.

I talked with Dr. Thomas Lewis, one of the book's authors and told him this happened to me over and over as I interviewed the centenarians. They told sad stories, I felt sad. They had deep memories about their childhoods, I felt contemplative. I went on journey with each of them. It was similar to falling in love, sharing those moments, a good feeling for me and for them, too.

Dr. Lewis explained this to me: There is nothing human beings want more than to have this experience with someone they care about. It's more important to us than wealth or status or great achievement. It's the one thing people want most.

So that's it — they wanted to talk, they needed to talk and I happened to be the listener. Who does not need a good heart-to-heart conversation, even with a stranger? It keeps us healthy. And so it is with the very oldest among us. If they are isolated, as many of them are, because they can't walk easily or see or hear — and they've lost their friends, their wives and husbands, and their children are far away — who is left? Go to a nursing home, an assisted living facility and you will find a person in need of a good, long talk.

That's it. Deep listening. It's simple, but not easy.

Ruth Ellis (no relation to me) was 100 years old when I met her and she knew she did not have long to live. Her one wish, after so many years on this earth, was for "some young person to take the time to visit with some older person."

We're all busy. We are distracted by our jobs, our responsibilities, the people who rely on us. We're all imperfect listeners.

But listening is a gift we can give to our seniors: Make the time to listen carefully, unselfishly, honestly.

MINDFUL HEALTH AND
THE POWER OF POSSIBILITY

Ellen J. Langer

f we exercised the control we actually have over our health and well-being, we'd find ourselves healthier and happier, and far less dependent on more formal systems of healthcare. This is true for all of us, but may be especially important for those over 70.

Imagine that you're 20 years younger. How do you feel? Well, if you're at all like the subjects in a provocative experiment my students and I conducted, you actually feel as if your body clock has been turned back two decades. We took a group of elderly men to an isolated New England retreat retrofit so that in every possible manner it appeared to be 20 years earlier. The men — in their late 70s and early 80s — spent a week there, having been told not to reminisce about the past, but to actually act as if they had traveled back in time. The idea was to see if changing the men's mindset about their age might lead to actual changes in health and fitness.

After just that one week, the men in the experimental group (compared with controls of the same age) had more joint flexibility, increased dexterity, improved vision and less arthritis in their hands. Their mental acuity had risen measurably, and they had improved

Ellen J. Langer is a professor in the Psychology Department at Harvard University. Her books written for general and academic readers include *Mindfulness, The Power of Mindful Learning, On Becoming An Artist,* and *Counterclockwise.* Langer has described her work on the illusion of control, aging, decision-making, and mindfulness theory in over 200 research articles and six academic books; and her experiments in social psychology have earned her inclusion in *The New York Times Magazine* "Year in Ideas" edition.

gait and posture. Outsiders who were shown the men's photographs judged them to be significantly younger than the controls. In other words, the aging process had in some measure been reversed.

Most of us live sealed in unlived lives, constrained by stereotypes we've adopted as truths. Once we shake loose from the negative clichés that dominate our thinking about health, we can mindfully open ourselves to possibilities for more productive lives no matter what our age. There's a great deal of hard science that backs up this assertion. Imagine if the eye chart at your optometrist's office was upside down, with the letters going from small to large rather than large to small. Would that have any effect on how you test? My lab looked at just this question. A standard eye chart — moving from large to small letters — creates the expectation that at some point you will be unable to read a line. When we turned the chart upside down, we reversed that expectation and people were able to read smaller letters than they could with standard charts. Their expectation — their mindset — improved their actual vision.

> Once we shake loose from the negative clichés that dominate our thinking about health, we can mindfully open ourselves to possibilities for more productive lives no matter what our age.

In another study, we considered how clothing can be a trigger for aging stereotypes. Most people try to dress appropriately for their age, so clothing in effect becomes a cue for ingrained attitudes about age. But what if this cue disappeared? We found that people who routinely wear uniforms as part of their work life, compared with people who dress in street clothes, missed fewer days owing to illness or injury, had fewer doctors' visits and hospitalizations, and had fewer chronic diseases — even though they all had the same socioeconomic status. This doesn't mean we should all start wearing uniforms. The point is that we are surrounded every day by subtle signals that aging is an undesirable period of decline. These signals make it difficult to continue developing a healthy mindset throughout adulthood.

Similar signals also lock all of us — regardless of age — into pigeonholes for disease. We are too quick to accept diagnostic categories like cancer, dementia and depression, and let them define us. Doing so preempts the possibility of a healthful future.

That's not to say that we won't encounter illness or bad moods — or that dressing like a teenager — will eliminate those things completely. But if we're open to the idea that the common beliefs we hold don't have to be correct, and begin exercising the control we have over our health, we just might feel as healthy as we did when we were younger.

So, how do we heal ourselves? First, we should take medical information about our health with a grain of salt. Medicine is not an exact science and only tells us what may be true for most people under the tested conditions, and may not be true for any of us individually. (None of us is the norm.) Second, realize that nothing stays the same. Even if we think we have some symptom — an ache, a loss of memory, depression, etc. — all the time, sometimes it's less than at other times and sometimes it's not there at all. We need to become aware of when it changes and ask why now and not then. In fact, for example, instead of solely attending to memory loss as we get older, we would benefit by noticing that most things are remembered quite well. Similarly, dyslexics read most words correctly and given that everything requires attention, those with ADHD are fine most of the time. Third, we need to recognize that full health is possible at every age and take small steps towards that healthy goal rather than accept helplessness. Fourth, while we are doing each of these, we should recognize that old age is not a disease and, if we become ill, we are not our diseases. They don't define us and they shouldn't limit our potential.

The world currently has been built by and for the young. Consider how ridiculous it would seem to conclude that a 25-year-old man's difficulty in riding a tricycle is due to an enlargement of his limbs and a loss of flexibility. Tricycles were not made with 25-year-olds in mind. When the 30-year-old is not interested in cartoons, we do not say he has a problem with paying attention. And when the 40-year-old forgets something, we don't jump to the diagnosis of senility.

Older adults are living in environments that were designed neither by them, nor for them. If we were to focus our attention on external reasons for perceived deficits, adapting the bicycle to the 25-year-old and not the other way around, we might decrease negative perceptions of the elderly and might encourage creative environmental solutions that benefit people of all ages.

Similarly, the elderly adult's mental capacities are often evaluated as if their desires, intentions and interests were equivalent to those of younger people. To return to 25-year-olds, it may also seem readily apparent to us that they don't care much about tricycles. However, such an analogy is rarely used to explain (or understand) the behavior of the elderly adult. When a child's parents cannot tell different cartoon characters apart or are unable to identify a top-forties hit from it's opening bars, the children do not conclude that their parents have lost either their ability to recognize faces or their memory for music. Rather, they conclude (correctly) that their parents don't care about Pokemon or Britney Spears. It is possible that older adults appear more forgetful, in part, simply because they do not care about the same things that younger people care about, including performance on memory tests. If an individual is told a piece of information, and does not care about remembering it, he or she may not encode that information in memory. If the person is later asked a question about the information and cannot answer it, has the information been forgotten? Information has to be learned in the first place before it later can be forgotten. Perhaps the elderly are not as forgetful as we assume; they may, in part, simply be more selective encoders.

Older people are often judged as if they are ascribing to the same set of values and reference points as those who judge them. For example, some researchers have suggested that in old age people naturally regress to a state of childhood. There is an important difference, however, between the resumption of behaviors that one exhibited in the past and the enactment of these behaviors for the first time. For example, if both a 7-year-old and a 97-year-old tell a dinner guest her stories are boring, they may be using the same words, but they are hardly exhibiting the same behavior. A mindful analysis would suggest that the child is uninhibited, meaning that he has not yet learned the socially appropriate response to dinner conversation. In contrast, the older adult is disinhibited. He is well aware of the norms of social behavior, but has chosen to ignore them. The observed similarity in the two behaviors creates a false equation of old age with childhood. People can't see beyond their own level of development so, perhaps not infrequently, the elderly adult is misunderstood.

It is possible that older adults appear more forgetful, in part, simply because they do not care about the same things that younger people care about, including performance on memory tests.

Based on our research, we need to focus our attention on:

a) the criteria used to evaluate the elderly (who decided and under what circumstances)

b) our inability to see past our own levels of development

c) the concept of change versus decay (focusing not on lowering performance standards, but on redefining them)

d) a more mindful approach to old age, both among the elderly and among those who stereotype them

A world that recognizes growth in late adulthood, encourages mindfulness for everyone. In several of our investigations over the past 30 years we've found that increasing mindfulness (without meditation) results in increased health and well-being as well as longevity.

There is probably no greater time of concern regarding diminished capacity, pain and disease than late adulthood. Nevertheless, this phase of our lives can still be one of growth. While many of the experienced debilities may be a natural part of aging, many are not and instead are a function of our mindsets about old age. It's time we learned to distinguish between the two. Once these impediments are removed, we'll see that we can enjoy a long, healthier and more fulfilling life, and that our own personal healthcare reform is a lot closer than many might think. ◉

HOW TO REDUCE AGEISM

⌐——— Erdman Palmore ———⌐

geism has been called the third "ism" — after racism and sexism. There is now general agreement that prejudice and discrimination against older people is wrong — just as racism and
sexism are wrong. However, there are two main differences between
ageism and the other "isms." First, we all are, or will be, vulnerable
to the effects of ageism — if we live long enough. So we all have a
personal stake in reducing ageism, regardless of our race or gender.

Ageism is not only wrong, it also reduces longevity in various
ways and contributes to the burden of healthcare for elders.
Furthermore, it makes elders ashamed of what they are and may
contribute to depression and other kinds of mental illness. So it is
vitally important to do what we can to reduce it and its effects.

The second difference is that because it is a recent concept, many
people are unaware of its prevalence and pernicious effects. Even
when they become aware of it, they are at a loss about what they can
do to reduce it.

There are two main strategies for reducing ageism: those focused
on the individual and those focused on changing the social structure.
Reducing individual ageism includes the following:

Erdman Palmore, Ph.D. was born in Japan of missionary parents. Since becoming a gerontologist at the Social Security Administration, he has been on a "mission" to increase
knowledge about aging and decrease ageism. He has published more than 100 articles
and chapters, as well as 15 books on aging. Since 1967 he has been a professor at the
Duke Center for the Study of Aging. He is now professor emeritus of medical sociology at
the Center.

- Testing for ageism — This is useful to determine what prejudices and misconceptions about aging the individual holds and need to be corrected. The "Facts on Aging Quiz" (Palmore, 1998) has been widely used for this purpose.

- Education, propaganda and exhortation — These are three related methods of trying to change the individual's attitudes and misconceptions.

- Slogans — These may be used to counteract the prejudices and misconceptions held by many people. Their advantage is that they are usually catchy and easy to remember. Examples are:
  - Age is just a number
  - Aging is living
  - Grow old with me, the best is yet to be
  - Old age is the consummation of life
  - Older is bolder
  - Aging is an *active* verb (Aging Services of California)
  - Youth is a gift; old age is a work of art

  (For more examples, see Palmore, Branch, & Harris, *Encyclopedia of Ageism,* 2005.)

- Benefits of aging — A list of these benefits may be used to counteract the negative stereotypes of aging.

- Religion — Religious organizations are uniquely able to use exhortation to reduce ageism.

- Media — Print and electronic media influence more people for more hours a day than any other one mass influence. It can be used to correct misconceptions, change images, and reduce stereotypes and discrimination.

- Personal contact — When personal contact is equal and cooperative, it is the most effective strategy for reducing any kind of prejudice.

- Models of successful aging—When elders themselves model successful aging by being healthy, active, involved and productive, they set examples that challenge the old negative stereotypes.

Social structures that need to be changed in order to reduce ageism include:

- Economy—Employment discrimination is probably the main type of economic discrimination that needs to be reduced. Also the positive forms of ageism, such as Supplemental Security Income (SSI) and Medicare, need to be reduced by extending their benefits to all ages.
- Government—Ageism in the government includes negative and positive aspects in various agencies and programs.
- Family—Ageism in the family includes norms against older women marrying younger men; norms against remarriage for widowed or divorced elders; and elder abuse by family members.
- Housing—Ageism in housing includes residential segregation and subsidized housing for elders only.

Personally, I am trying to do what I can to reduce ageism in the following ways:

- Research—I continue to do research on ageism through my "Facts on Aging Quiz" (FAQ), Ageism Survey, Relating to Older Persons Evaluation (ROPE), and Health Behavior Inventory. The FAQ remains the only published document to test of basic knowledge and misconceptions about aging. The Ageism Survey asks older people which kinds of ageism they personally have experienced. The ROPE questionnaire asks people to identify their ageist actions (negative and positive) when relating to older people. The Health Behavior Inventory asks people to report their healthy behaviors (such as exercise), as well as their unhealthy behaviors that are attempts to deny their age (such as dying their hair, using Botox, etc.) I consider these denial behaviors as resulting from ageism in our culture.

- Writing — I have published the textbook *Ageism* (Palmore, E.B., 1990) and more recently *The Encyclopedia of Ageism (2005).* I also write occasional editorials in our Duke Center on Aging newsletter, *The Center Report.*

- Personal fitness — I do exercises and weightlifting all year long and keep my weight down to stay fit (my "battle of the bulge"). I ride my bicycle to my office at Duke (20 miles round trip) twice a week (unless it's inclement or over 90 degrees). I think bike riding and hiking are two of my main joys in life ... as well as riding my motor scooter.

- Proving you can improve with age — Each year before my birthday, I increase my endurance so I can ride my age on my bicycle and do my age in push-ups, sit-ups and knee-bends (this year, 80). This also gives me great satisfaction, as well as being an annual challenge.

- Birthday adventure — Each year I also celebrate my birthday by doing some "adventure" to challenge the stereotype that old men are frail, timid and uninteresting. Some of my favorite adventures: tandem sky-diving, hang-gliding, bungee-jumping, white-water rafting, hot-air ballooning, glider riding and getting tattoos. I now have three tattoos: the "Happy Humanist" logo (a figure with arms over head that forms an "H"), the Unitarian-Universalist logo (two overlapping circles with a flaming chalice in the middle), and the United Nations logo (the world framed with laurel leaves). Some older siblings did not like the tattoos, but most friends (especially those under 65) seemed to think they are "cool." The most common question: "Did it hurt?" Answer: "Yes."

This year's adventure was an "indoor sky-dive" in which you jump into a big vertical wind tunnel that propels you up or down, twirling to the left or right, depending on how you hold you arms and legs — just like real sky-diving.

All the other adventures were thrilling or at least pleasant. The tandem sky-dive was the most thrilling. The 45 seconds of free-fall were the most thrilling 45 seconds of my life.

> **So I brag about my age every chance I get — even though that may be "reverse ageism" or "positive ageism."**

- Pointing out examples — I'm afraid I can be boring the way I harp on examples of ageism in the language and attitudes of friends and family.

- Longevity — "The best revenge is outliving your enemies," they say. I don't really have any enemies, but it would be nice to keep enjoying life for many more years.

- Being proud of your age — Many people are ashamed of their age. They either won't tell you their age or they lie about their age. I've known people who won't even celebrate their birthdays. I think this is clearly a form of ageism. I don't know what the best way is to convince people that they should be proud of their age, rather than ashamed of it. I'm afraid we may have to change the whole culture and/or try to educate a new generation on the advantages and promise of greater longevity. So I brag about my age every chance I get — even though that may be "reverse ageism" or "positive ageism." And I celebrate my birthdays in various ways as described above. These celebrations are also powerful motivators for me to keep in shape, so I can keep celebrating in these ways.

I don't know whether I'll live to be 100 (and ride 100 miles), but so far so good!

References

- Palmore, E.B. (1998). *Facts on Aging Quiz* (*2nd Ed.*). New York, Springer.
- Palmore, E.B., Branch, L., & Harris, D.K. (Eds.). (2005). *The Encyclopedia of Ageism*. New York: Routledge.
- Palmore, E.B. (1990). *Ageism: Negative and Positive*. New York: Springer.

COGNITION, MEMORY AND WISDOM

⸻ Gene D. Cohen, M.D ⸻

O n a table in a high-ceilinged room in the Museum of Georgia in the former Soviet Republic, sits a hollow-eyed skull. The skull is not as mute as it may appear. To the anthropologists who unearthed it, the skull whispers messages about the importance of the elderly in ancient protohuman societies. This skull is the earliest known evidence of the emergence roughly 1.8 million years ago of a powerful new force in the evolution of human beings: wisdom.

The anthropologists at the museum refer to the skull as "the old man," even though they estimate that the hominid — a member of the *Homo erectus* species — was about 40 when he died. Indeed, all the other skulls found in the same stratum of soil appear much smoother, with small, graceful features and intact teeth, indicating a younger age at death. Reaching 40 in that time was probably equivalent to reaching the century mark today. But the stunning thing about "the old man" is this: Not only does he have no teeth, but the tooth sockets are smooth, filled in with bone that grew over the

Gene D. Cohen, M.D., Ph.D., served as director of the Center on Aging, Health & Humanities at George Washington University, where he also held the positions of professor of health care sciences and professor of psychiatry. He served as the first chief of the Center on Aging at the National Institute of Mental Health and acting director of the National Institute on Aging. Dr. Cohen authored *The Creative Age* and *The Mature Mind*.

Dr. Cohen passed away in November 2009. This posthumous contribution honors his desire to participate in this project and his invaluable contributions to the field of aging. The text is excerpted from The Mature Mind: The Power of the Aging Brain. *Copyright 2005 by Gene Cohen, M.D., Ph.D. Published by Basic Books.*

spaces. This bone regrowth shows that "the old man" lived several years after his teeth fell out. At a time when hominids were very likely as often prey as predators, the most plausible explanation of this curious feature is that he was helped by his fellows — he was fed and cared for. And this, in turn, means that he was valued.

Clearly, when it comes to human beings, the capacities to teach; to transmit wisdom and skills, and to serve as a repository for the culture are just as important as the capacity to reproduce.

We cannot know what this "old man" contributed to his community, but most plausibly he was valuable because of what he *knew*. Although pinpointing the origins of language will never be an exact science (sounds leave no fossils), available evidence about brain size and the structure of rib cages leads some anthropologists to suggest that *Homo erectus*, and maybe even the earlier *Homo habilis*, were capable of producing some form of language. It may have been the invention and use of language, in fact, that was the decisive factor in the success of *Homo erectus* over the other hominid species alive at the same time, such as the Neanderthals. In any case, the ability to transmit knowledge from one generation to another must have been an enormous asset and, as a consequence, would have raised the value of those members of a community who had accumulated the most knowledge — the elders — and were able to transmit it to others.

As the body of human knowledge grew over the ages, and as the social and cultural life of our species became more complex, the value of older adults increased as well. This is why natural selection has favored a relatively long human life span despite the fact that the female reproduction potential typically ends in the late 40s. Clearly, when it comes to human beings, the capacities to teach; to transmit wisdom and skills, and to serve as a repository for the culture are just as important as the capacity to reproduce. The complexity of today's global society and the variety of skills required to master those complexities only amplify the importance of the older adults among us.

Wisdom

What exactly is wisdom, and how does it develop? One standard definition is that wisdom consists of "making the best use of available knowledge." This rather utilitarian approach implies that wisdom requires specific knowledge as well as a broad understanding of the context in which that knowledge can be put to use. But this definition isn't completely satisfying. For most people, wisdom also connotes a perspective that supports the long-term common good over the short-term good for an individual. Insights and acts that many people agree are wise tend to be grounded in past experience or history and yet can anticipate likely future consequences. Wise acts, in other words, look both backward and forward. Wisdom is also generally understood to be informed by multiple forms of intelligence — reason, intuition, heart and spirit. It is fundamentally the manifestation of developmental intelligence — a mature integration of thinking skills, emotional intelligence, judgment, social skills and life experience.

Better Social Choices with Aging

The existential philosopher Albert Camus once commented, "Life is a sum of all your choices." In J. K. Rowling's book *Harry Potter and the Chamber of Secrets*, Hogwarts headmaster Aldus Dumbledore (one of the best depictions of positive aging in modern children's literature) advises young Harry: "It is our choices that show what we truly are, far more than our abilities." Maturing social intelligence contributes to better choices in every sphere of one's life, particularly in one's social life.

With age we are often more discriminating about our relationships. Research shows that older adults more readily sever superficial or unsatisfying relationships in order to spend their time with people they care about and with whom they feel comfortable and able to freely express their true selves. As one 70-year-old woman told me, "Life is too short for me to put up with people I don't feel good being around."

Social intelligence also helps improve conflict resolution skills. Studies show that older adults use a combination of coping and negotiating strategies that lead to greater impulse control and the tendency to more effectively appraise conflict-charged situations, which results in more effective, satisfying choices of action. This is one reason that age is an asset in many people-orientated occupations such as manager, judge, politician, and diplomat.

BENEFITS OF AN AGING SOCIETY

———— Harry (Rick) Moody ————

An "aging society" is a society experiencing the demographic process known as "population aging:" that is, an increased proportion of the old and a decreased relative proportion of the young.

Most nations of the world, including less developed countries, are experiencing population aging, but population aging is most advanced in industrialized countries of Western Europe, North America and Japan. The United States, at latest report, is showing a population increase, both because of increased fertility and immigration. Still, because of the aging of Boomers, the proportion of the United States over age 65 will rise from about 13 percent to nearly 20 percent. Thus, the United States, too, is experiencing population aging, like other advanced industrialized countries.

Fear of an Aging Society

There is fear about population aging, because of belief that an aging population: 1) costs too much (health and welfare expenditures); 2) is less productive; 3) is less creative; and 4) is likely to have slower economic growth. These fears need to be addressed in factual terms.

Harry (Rick) Moody directs the AARP Office of Academic Affairs. He is a gerontological educator and ethicist and also serves as senior associate with the International Longevity Center-USA and as senior fellow with Civic Ventures. He has several books, including *Ethics in an Aging Society* and the textbook now in its sixth edition, *Aging: Concepts and Controversies.*

Cost is often understood in terms of the so-called dependency ratio or transfer payments from workers to non-workers. Yet, the cost of pensions — public or private — vary dramatically if people work longer, as is beginning to happen today. The agenda of so-called "productive aging" suggests that an older population could actually offer benefits, if work-life extension were combined with retraining, lifelong learning and better use of accumulated human capital.

Economists remind us that rates of economic productivity depend much more on capital investment (including human capital) and technology, than other factors. There is a stereotype that links creativity exclusively with youth. But, research by Gene Cohen in his book *The Mature Mind*, has cast doubt on such linkage. The topic is debated in the gerontological literature that documents cognitive deficits with advancing age. The benefits of life experience have been far less studied. Rates of economic growth depend on a variety of factors, including capital investment, trade, savings rates, technology and diffusion of innovation. Population aging, by itself, need not entail slower economic growth, but is likely to promote a shift of economic resources toward so-called "Silver Industries" that will grow faster with an older population (e.g., healthcare, financial services, retirement housing, and travel and hospitality).

In sum, the costs of an aging society (population aging) are by no means invariant or something to be feared. Robert N. Butler, M.D. in *The Longevity Revolution*, among others, points to the economic impact of longevity, especially if longer life is linked to greater health — as in recent decades. The so-called "compression of morbidity" hypothesis remains an open question. Longer life can present longer periods of dependency, but it also has brought longer periods of potentially healthy, active and productive life. Again, this potential for productive aging will only be fulfilled if institutional changes take place (e.g., reducing age discrimination, extending work-life, human capital investment through retraining and lifelong learning over the entire life-course, and so on).

Benefits of an Aging Society

Discussion of the "benefits of an aging society" tends to be limited to the topics of healthcare and work-life. Other factors are typically overlooked, such as dimensions of human exchange not captured by "monetized" exchange in the marketplace. This includes volunteerism, family caregiving and civic engagement, among others. Later life can also be a time for Lars Tornstam's idea of "gero-transcendence" and cultivating values — generativity and wisdom, for example — overlooked by modern societies. Finally, population aging and population shrinkage offer us a path toward reducing the environmental impact of the human species on the planet.

Finally, population aging and population shrinkage offer us a path toward reducing the environmental impact of the human species on the planet

Because such benefits are overlooked, they are not measured or documented, and little research is done to link potential benefits to policy goals. For example, attending religious services, volunteering or supporting the arts are sometimes "justified" because they contribute, allegedly, to better health outcomes. Such claims are debatable, but even if true, "better health" is not why individuals support religion, volunteer roles or the arts. As Albert Einstein said, "Not everything that counts can be counted."

There is also the problem of introducing what Karl Marx called the "cash nexus" into family life: for example, paying for family caregiving. Whatever the values of permitting family members to be paid, we need to avoid making money be the measure of all values.

Increased attention to productivity may make us overlook the benefits of people having greater leisure in retirement. One reason is that the use of leisure time has been poorly organized. The biggest use of free time among retired people is watching TV, which is associated with poor health and isolation. But one can imagine an aging society where the benefits of leisure are much greater.

Modern societies overvalue activity, compared to contemplation or detachment, argues Tornstam. But contemporary gerontology tends to hold "disengagement" in disfavor. Religion and spirituality can help us think more critically about what makes us human and what gives life meaning. As the saying goes, "Nobody on their deathbed ever said, I wish I'd spent more time on my business."

Finally, there are benefits associated with population aging that pertain to our global environment. There is evidence that older people may be less interested in buying more and less tuned in to consumerism as a way of life. Environmentalists could celebrate an aging population for receptivity to "green" purchasing goals.

When we step back and think about aging and the challenge of the global environment, especially climate change, it becomes clear that all of our environmental problems would be easier to address if the world population were, say, 3 billion and not 7 billion people. Greater longevity is not an environmental threat because we do not reasonably expect billions of people to be centenarians. We can reasonably expect societies where smaller numbers of children are cared for with greater attention; and we can expect greater investment in human capital, reinforced by the expectation of longer lives and longer "payback" of investments in childhood and youth. This approach is consistent with the "life course perspective" about human aging.

An environmentally sustainable world is a world where population aging is matched by cultivation of the benefits of an aging society. Civic Ventures' Marc Freedman said it well in describing an older population as our only indefinitely renewable natural resource. Population aging is not a threat, but an opportunity. Without this optimism, we may not summon the strength to make those changes we need to make use of the opportunity before us, both as individuals and as a species. But history is not fixed and the choice is ours. ⬤

GENERATIONAL NONSENSE

└───── David Wolfe ─────┘

"The play is always the same. Only the actors change." If you are over 40, chances are you'll understand a middle-aged friend's meaning when he said, "More and more, when I look in the mirror to shave each morning, I see my father."

We spend about half of our lives — the first half — thinking that our generation is quite different than our parents' generation. But in the second half of life, many of us begin realizing that the people of one generation live out their lives not all that much different from people in previous generations.

Marketers are big on spelling out alleged generational differences. They try to impress potential clients with their special insights into this or that generation. Truth be told, however, there is a lot of nonsense swirling around in conversations about generations.

Of course there are differences between my generation and my parents' generation. However, most of those differences are cosmetic. They don't spell fundamental differences in what people want from life. My parents wanted pretty much the same thing from life that I've wanted at comparable ages. One telling difference, of course, is I have had more options available to me to express my life. Both my parents grew up with outhouses and no electricity. They got around

---

David Wolfe is an international authority on consumer behavior in the second half of life. He is the author of *Ageless Marketing: Strategies for Reaching the Hearts and Minds of the New Customer Majority* and *Firms of Endearment: How World-Class Companies Profit from Passion and Purpose.*

in buckboards until the early 1920s. But those differences did not translate into differences in basic needs and wants.

Looking at the issue from a *Maslovian* perspective, I can't imagine Maslow saying, for example, "Boomers' needs are different from the five levels of basic human needs in my hierarchy of basic needs." Basic needs do not change from one generation to the next. And it seems to me that the first thing a marketer wants to know in some depth is about people's basic needs.

Having raised three Boomers, two Gen X'ers and one Gen Y'er (Millennial), I can attest to each of my six children going through the same stages of development. While their behavioral styles differed, the drivers of their behavior did not. What they were looking for in life as teens is the same thing I was looking for as a teen.

The nonsense about generations begins with arbitrarily defining a generation in numbers of years. No one seems to notice, but the birthing years of Boomers, Gen X'ers and Millennials span a differing number of years depending on the source.

While most people say Boomers were born between 1946 and 1964, some say the first Boomer was born in 1943. The last birthing year of Boomers to some minds is 1956. The birthing years for Generation X are usually marked as 1965 to 1982, but some extend their birthing years to the end of the first Reagan term of office.

On the first page of a recent Google search, eight out of the first 20 sources disagreed on the number of Millennials. The population count ranged from 70 million to 100 million. A sampling of the calendared bookends of the Millennial cohort as indicated by the first 20 Google listings: 1984-1993 (9 years); 1982-1998 (16 years); 1982-2001 (19 years); and 1982-2003 (21 years).

It is astonishing that hardly anyone seems bothered by such intellectual sloppiness. There is one thing I have noticed in people's claims about the size of generations: Those who have a vested interest in a particular generation tend to define that generation by the greatest number of birthing years. They may have written a book on the generation. More commonly they have a consulting practice focused on that generation. The claim that a given generation is the "biggest generation in history" is commonplace. Just increase the number of birthing years and it's easy to make such a claim.

When my daughter Stephanie was seven, she looked up from the comics one morning at breakfast and asked me to listen to her as she read the "Calvin and Hobbes" strip. It seems that Calvin was complaining to his imaginary tiger friend that "they" don't name a generation "until you get really old — like 20." Stephanie then said with a quizzical look on her face, "Daddy, I don't understand. Isn't a new generation born every day?"

At age seven she had pointed out the obvious that probably few in marketing will ever get. While conducting a workshop in 1996, the year the first Boomers turned 50, I asked for two volunteers, one born in 1946 and another born in 1964, the bookends of the "Boomer Generation." A balding man, a bit wide of girth, approached the podium. A trim, well-groomed 32-year-old man followed him. Before I could say anything, someone from the audience got the point and shouted, "They're twins!"

I asked each man to talk about his plans for the next five years. The 32-year-old said he wanted to get into the top echelons of his company, buy a bigger house and start raising a family. The 50-year old said, in effect, "Been there, done that. I'm easin' up now. Making my life simple. Gonna retire in a few years and I'd like to start getting some practice now."

Each man was at a different stage of life, with different aspirations and goals; yet both are called Boomers, supposedly having much in common because, we're told over and over, "Boomers were shaped by the same events growing up."

In his book, *The Seasons of a Man's Life,* Yale developmental psychologist Daniel Levinson drafted a definition of *generation* that makes more sense than much of what we hear in marketing about what defines this or that generation. Levinson found that in terms of a person's tight affinity with others — certainly a prerequisite of the theory of cohort effect — a generation consists of people within six or seven years of one another. Thus, from a *subjective* perspective, the *psychological* span of a generation is 12 to 14 years.

Let's apply Levinson's thinking to the so-called Boomer Generation that spans 18 years. As was evident in the differences between the two Boomers in my workshop, the oldest and youngest Boomers fall into two separate generations.

Because cohort effects supposedly give people who feel generationally connected certain like-mindedness, Levinson's research challenges much of what has been said about Boomers. Specifically, given his claim that generational affinity applies to people within six or seven years of one's age, it is nonsensical to talk about the *Boomer market* as though it were one monolithic market. Because, they did not all grow up experiencing the same seminal events. For example, the youngest Boomers were toddlers when Bobby Kennedy and Martin Luther King were murdered.

By Levinson's reasoning, babies born between 1946 and 1952 had one foot in the so-called Silent Generation and the other in the Boomer Generation. Babies born between 1958 and 1964 had one foot in the Boomer Generation and the other foot in Generation X. Only people born between 1952 and 1958, numbering around 25 million (not 78 million) had both feet in the Boomer Generation as most people define it.

It is no secret that how you frame a challenge predisposes how you will meet that challenge. Currently, challenges concerning aging Boomers are being framed largely within the context of how different Boomers are from members of previous generations of older people. It is a shallow approach to say the least and stands in the way of meeting their deeper needs — needs that are characteristic of people of any generation at a comparable stage of life. Avoiding such an inadequacy requires a better understanding of adult development in later life than is commonplace in the marketing, academic and public policy circles where older people are the primary consumer focus. A wonderful place to start is the late Gene Cohen's last book, *The Mature Mind.* He did not speak of generations. He looked at older people in terms of developmental milestones that mark their journey towards being all they can be. That is not a generational attribute. It is a stage of life attribute as old as man.

I'M OLD.

Maria Dwight

'm old. I am 75, which through no stretch of the imagination can be considered "middle aged" and certainly isn't young. Ergo: I must be old. I am not young-old, also euphemistically known as "an active adult." I am not "a frail elder" either and probably have a decade before I hit that benchmark. So, I am just plain old.

There is nothing wrong with being old. I still work 50 hours-a-week at a career that I love. I don't always make my bed before I go to the office, and often leave the dishes in the sink, but I still do the *Times* crossword puzzle, to keep away the dreaded brain atrophy, as much as for pleasure. I eat well (sometimes, I must admit to peanut butter-folded over, over the sink). I kayak, get undressed and dressed in the security lines within the three-minute allotted timeframe, put my own suitcase in the overhead bin, and other miscellaneous exercises. I am very careful to take my vitamins, eat leafy green stuff and make sure that I drink the prescribed red wine for a healthy heart.

I must look 75 since the only nips and tucks in my body were followed by radiation, none of which are enhancing procedures. My chin and my neck have slowly become one. My waist must be somewhere between my breasts and my hips, but no longer invites a

Maria Dwight is president of Gerontological Services, Inc. (GSI), a market research and strategic planning firm in Santa Monica, California. She inadvertently entered the field of gerontology in 1966, as a welfare commissioner whose duties included oversight of the municipal home, the former *poor farm* of Holyoke, Massachusetts. It has been her passion ever since. She stopped sky diving some time ago, but is still looking for adventures. In the near future she hopes to use her expertise in helping the Buddhist community develop a retirement haven for monks in Bhutan.

glittery belt and only seeks refuge under layers of tunics, capes or sweatshirts left behind by forgetful adolescent grandsons.

I am no longer carded at the movies.

I am old, but I am also very lucky. I am one of the 12 percent of women over 65 who have a job, so I have health insurance as well as Medicare. This means it is not a struggle to find a doctor who "will see me now." I am in good health, in spite of myself. I have a good education. My children are happy with their lives and are self-sufficient. I have an annual income over the ($16k!) median of a "white," "widowed" female. I own a house whose mortgage will long outlive me. I was frugal and tucked away my savings, only to have them evaporate in the last couple of years. But I still have enough to live comfortably, unlike many of my age peers. The early lessons of a depression-era childhood have held me in good stead. "Use it up, make it do, do without" was the mantra, along with "Turn off the lights!"

So now I am working on becoming a female curmudgeon.

I can't seem to find new movies that interest me. Spare me the retirement communities' staples of Fred Astaire and Ginger Rogers. Save me from the dreary reruns on PBS of passé rockers and crooners, and I couldn't stand Lawrence Welk the first time around. Why are movies so dreadfully loud, rude and gratuitously crude? Who are these young women, like cloned Barbie Dolls, who seem to have forgotten to put on anything over their underwear? And their wannabes of all sizes, shapes and ages who frequent my supermarket, with their tattooed bulges on display? And their beaus, conversely in clothes that are far too large and hang, often precariously and sometimes unsuccessfully, off their hips, sharing with us the brand of their boxer shorts.

What's with the compulsion to be on the cell phone? The plane lands and everyone turns on their phones to tell the world, in a chorus, that they just landed. So? People walk through stores and down streets talking to air. Are they mentally ill or just impolite?

What is with this glorification of "multi-tasking"? I was taught (often unsuccessfully) to do one thing at a time and do it well. But I also was taught to save for a rainy day, to stand when older people entered the room, to not interrupt, to make my bed with hospital corners, to write thank you notes, to watch my language, to not take the biggest cookie on the plate and to chew with my mouth closed.

So, I am old. I am one of the "Silent Generation" that was squeezed between the "Greatest" and the "Boomers." Our war was Korea. We came from small families and we spawned large ones. We believed in "togetherness" and "at home moms." We volunteered in our communities and behaved ... until we didn't. Then we led the most pervasive changes for social justice in our nation's history. It is our generation that crossed the bridge at Selma; marched on Washington, D.C.; rode the Freedom Buses; opened the doors for the Feminist Movement; fought back at Stonewall Inn; landed on the moon in Apollo 11; and redefined art, poetry and theater. Elvis Presley was among the "Silents" and that boy could howl and he could rock!

So, keep on howling! Rock on, all you old people! Keep changing the world, or at least your part of it. Don't forget about others who are old and keep their needs in the faces of the politicians and the bureaucrats. Show all the younger generations what it means to be "Old and proud of it!"

MATHEMATICAL

FROM POPULATION BOMB TO
LONGEVITY REVOLUTION

└──────── Theodore Roszak ──·──────┐

R emember "Year Six Billion"? That was the campaign the United
Nations launched in December 1999, when it estimated that the
six-billionth person was born somewhere on the planet. Year Six
Billion was a familiar part of its long-standing call for worldwide population control. The pictures that accompanied the campaign were the
familiar heart-breaking horrors of famine and disease raging through
Africa, Asia and Latin America: starving babies, emaciated mothers
and elders staring bleakly out at the world.

At the same time the UN was filling the media with all the human
miseries that have been at the head of the environmental agenda since
the days of Paul Ehrlich's population bomb, Japanese workers were being offered a new way to become millionaires. A million yen, that
is — roughly $10,000 American. All they have to do is start having ba-
bies. For every baby after the family's second child, the company will
pay the bonus.

Japan, the oldest society in history with a record-breaking average
age now past 40, thinks it needs more people, not less — especially
young people. Bandai is not alone in trying to raise the national birth
rate; it is simply offering a fatter incentive than other companies —

Theodore Roszak is professor of history emeritus at California State University, East Bay. He
is the author of *The Making of a Counterculture* (1969). His most recent book is *The Making of an Elder Culture: Reflections on the Future of America's Most Audacious Generation*,
published by New Society Publishers, 2009.

perhaps because it has a more vested interest. Bandai makes Power Ranger toys and virtual pets. To remain at zero-growth, a nation's fertility rate has to stand at 2.1. At the current Japanese rate of 1.38, Bandai sees its customer base diminishing by the year.

What Bandai and other employers are offering is now supplemented by official educational and child-care subsidies aimed at boosting the size of families. Japan is not alone in pressing toward pronatalist policies. The Germans are offering similar subsidies. The Czechs are running anti-contraception ads advising couples to "stop taking care." (Billboard ads show Johan Sebastian Bach as 20 naked clones.) A leading science magazine calls the "birth dearth" across Europe the "population bombshell" that poses the greatest threat to prosperity. In less than 50 years, world population growth has slowed from 2.2 percent annually to 1.4 percent. According to World Watch Institute, never one to underplay an environmental issue, among industrial societies, which are the highest consumers and worst environmental predators, 70 nations are at or approaching zero-population growth.

So much moral passion has been invested in population politics over the past three decades that one feels churlish even to hint at the possibility that the population bomb is being defused.

Despite the birth of that six-billionth person in 1999, figures like these have led the United Nations to revise its over-all projection for world population. Its best-case estimate, which an increasing number of demographers now take seriously, predicts that world population will peak in 2040 at 8 to 9 billion, then shrink back steadily over the next century and a half. If fertility rates continue to fall, by 2150, the planet's population could drop as low as 3.6 billion.

So much moral passion has been invested in population politics over the past three decades that one feels churlish even to hint at the possibility that the population bomb is being defused. In every society it touches — including China and India — industrialism is releasing social and biological forces that work to restrain population growth.

All this is not to say that population is off the environmental agenda. The issue has, however, changed its shape radically. Where the miseries of overpopulation once seemed to be our demographic nemesis, some commentators now believe an ominous new prospect has arisen in the very societies that have achieved zero-growth. There they see a *longevity revolution* in progress that points toward a radical reorientation in the political and economic relations between young and old. Life expectancy, which has never been seen as a significant factor in population politics, has now become an urgent concern.

And global longevity may only be in its opening phase. Up to this point in modern history, the greatest gains in life expectancy have resulted from three compounding factors: public health, improving nutrition and steady advances in medical science. Spectacular as these achievements have been, they pale in comparison with what the new field of biotechnology promises to offer. Writing in the *Journal of the American Medical Association* in October 1997, the biotechnicians Dwayne Banks and Michael Fossel have called for a review of all public policy based upon conventional population projections. "The possibility of extending the maximum human life span," they warn, "has gone from legend to laboratory. Predictions of the costs of aging will be hollow unless they factor in the ongoing, nascent and fundamental changes in our understanding of aging and age-related diseases."

Now that we have at least the hint of a more hopeful demographic future, conservative economists, who have tended to be as dismal about population issues as Malthus once was, are hardly cheered by what they see ahead. Indeed, they are gloomier than ever. Just as their ideological forebears warned that the dole would impoverish the nation, conservative think tanks today insist that senior entitlements will do the same. In their eyes, the "rise of the wrinklies" looms as a major threat to the global economy. In the view of Ben Wattenberg of the American Enterprise Institute, aging is "the real population bomb." As Wattenberg puts it, "I am not a catastrophe-monger, but it is a hell of a lot bigger problem than too many people."

But the longevity revolution may be buttressed in ways that go beyond senior voting power. Demographers are standing Malthus on his head. Fertility and life expectancy may be inextricably linked in ways that are only now becoming apparent. In the long run, it may be biologically and sociologically impossible to expect a Baby Boom from long-lived societies. A recent study of the English aristocracy over a thousand years of history indicates the same demographic pattern we find in other species. The study published in *Nature* in December 1998 shows that parents—both mothers and fathers—who were barren or produced the fewest progeny lived longer than more prolific members of their class. This corroborates a 1997 study indicating that American women who waited until they were in their forties to have their first—and usually only—child had a far better chance of reaching 100. In brief, *fertility is inversely correlated with life expectancy.*

This may be the underlying reason why the industrial nations seem to be making what demographic analyst Joel Cohen calls "Methuselah's choice," a near stationery population based on long life and low reproduction. There may, however, be no "choice" here at all, but rather the expression of a new law of population that could not be recognized until the world had produced so many "wrinklies."

Some analysts have characterized these preferences as a matter of parents having a refrigerator instead of a baby. As flippant as that sounds, global aging is inextricably connected with the values of the young — especially young women. The longevity revolution, far from being a geriatric conspiracy, results from intergenerational choices. Young and old, we are all in it together. It is due as much to what the young want (smaller families) as to what the old need (better healthcare.) Entitlements are the long-term cost of the values for which young and old alike are spontaneously opting everywhere.

Nobody saw it coming, but at its highest stage of development, industrial society becomes a healthcare economy. Within the next generation, we may view the interests of patients the way we once viewed the interests of motorists when we were a young, mobile, automotive society spreading into the suburbs. Then nobody questioned the necessity of investing trillions in automobiles, highways and gasoline.

But there will be a difference. In contrast to other economic priorities like automobiles, high-tech or aerospace, the life-and-death necessities of an aging population are as ethically defensible and environmentally benign as human needs can become. Gas-guzzling cars, TV dinners, electronic gadgetry, even the taste for well-marbled beef that turned fertile acreage into pasture — all could be identified as unconscionable extravagance. But, investing in good health is not only morally tenable, it actually weighs far more lightly on the planet. Taken together with the less-than-zero population growth that a longer life expectancy brings with it, the longevity revolution may at last offer industrial civilization the preconditions for sustainable prosperity. Or, to put it another way, longevity might be the true wealth of nations. ◉

MAPPING THE GROWTH OF OLDER AMERICA

⊢———— William H. Frey ————⊣

G rowing public attention is focused on the national implications of the impending "age tsunami" about to hit America's
older population. After minimal growth in the 1990s, and
modest gains during this past decade, the U.S. senior population will
begin to mushroom when the leading edge of the huge Baby Boom
Generation — born between 1946 and 1965 — reaches age 65 in the
year 2011.

The consumer patterns, family choices, and social and economic
needs of tomorrow's "Boomer seniors" will likely differ sharply from
senior proclivities of the past. After all, as this unique generation of
over 80 million Americans plowed its way through the nation's school
systems, labor market, housing market and stock market, it
continually broke the mold, transforming both public and private
institutions in its path.

Any discussion of a changing senior population must also include
the World War II generation — born between 1936 and 1945 — whose
members are currently entering the 65-and-older category. They,
too, contrast with their preceding generation. Not only are they more

Demographer William H. Frey is a senior fellow with The Brookings Institution's Metropolitan Policy Program where he specializes in issues involving urban populations, migration,
immigration, race, aging, political demographics and the U.S. Census. He is the author of
"Mapping the Growth of Older America: Seniors and Boomers in the Early 21st Century"
(a publication of The Brookings Institutions' Living Cities Series), from which this article
is excerpted by permission. He is also a research professor in population studies at the
University of Michigan.

numerous than the Depression-era cohort, but also they benefited tremendously from the economic prosperity that followed the war: rising home ownership, steady job growth and improved access to education. As newly minted seniors in the current decade, this generation bridges the retirees born during the Depression and the impending Boomer seniors.

GROWTH IN U.S., TOTAL AND SENIOR POPULATIONS BY DECADE, 1970-2030

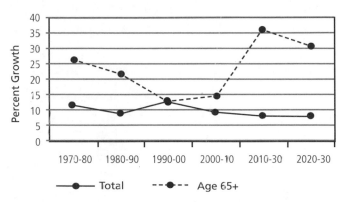

Source: Author's analysis of U.S. decennial censuses and Census Bureau Population Projections

Just as these new and emerging seniors reshape the national social, political and economic scene, they will exert profound impacts at the local level, too. Almost all parts of the country will be gaining seniors faster in the future than in the recent past, but the magnitude and characteristics of senior growth will vary widely from place to place. In many cases, areas previously known for their youthful populations — especially the Sun Belt and the suburbs — will undergo the most rapid senior growth.

The Brookings Institution report "Mapping the Growth of Older America: Seniors and Boomers in the Early 21st Century," published in May 2007, maps future changes in America's senior population as upcoming generations both migrate and "age-in-place" — that is, grow older in their existing locations — across the national landscape.

Analysis of U.S. Census Bureau data on the changing size, location and characteristics of America's senior (aged 65 and over) and
pre-senior (aged 55 to 64) populations reveals that:

**The aging of the Baby Boom Generation makes pre-seniors
this decade's fastest-growing age group, expanding nearly 50 percent in size from 2000 to 2010.** Poised to create a "senior tsunami"
beginning in 2011, this group will be more highly educated, have
more professional women, and exhibit more household diversity
than previous generations entering traditional retirement age.

POPULATION CHANGE BY AGE COHORT, UNITED STATES, 2000-10

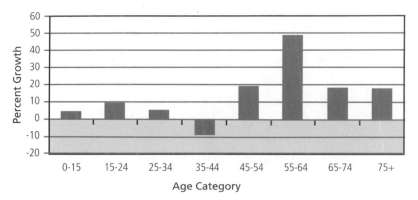

Source: Author's analysis of U.S. decennial censuses and Census Bureau Population Projections

**Pre-senior populations are growing rapidly everywhere,
especially in economically dynamic Sun Belt areas previously
known for their youth, such as Las Vegas, Austin, Atlanta and
Dallas.** "Exurban" parts of these large metro areas, along with smaller
metro areas like Santa Fe, New Mexico, and Boise, Idaho, seem to
have attracted mobile Boomers who wish to live near both work and
natural amenities as they approach retirement age.

**The World War II generation, currently entering its senior
years, is growing fastest in the Intermountain West and South**

Atlantic states, especially suburban areas there. These high-growth areas tend to have younger, higher-income, more highly-educated senior populations. Despite their low rates of senior growth, northern states like Pennsylvania, Iowa and North Dakota exhibit some of the nation's highest senior population shares due to low immigration and past out-migration of their younger residents.

In states where senior populations will grow fastest over the next 35 years, "aging-in-place," rather than migration, will drive this growth. In Georgia, for instance, the senior population will increase by more than 40 percent from 2010 to 2020 due to the aging of existing residents, versus less than 3 percent due to migration.

Projected Boomer aging will cause the suburbs of New York, Philadelphia, Chicago and Los Angeles to become considerably "older" than the cities themselves by 2040. Seniors and pre-seniors moving from cities to suburbs outnumber those moving in the opposite direction; those moving into cities are, on average, more highly educated, more affluent and less likely to be married than their suburbanizing counterparts.

Today's seniors and pre-seniors are upending traditional notions of how and where Americans spend their later years. The rise of Boomer populations in suburban and Sun Belt locations will create new demand for senior-oriented housing and amenities. However, as older populations age-in-place — especially in the suburbs of slower-growing metropolitan areas — public policies must respond to the new stresses they will exert on health, transportation and social-support systems.

Universal Growth, New Challenges

The 2007 survey, on which the Brookings Institution's report "Mapping the Growth of Older America: Seniors and Boomers in the

Early 21st Century" is based, provides an overview of current and future geographic shifts of America's senior and pre-senior populations, with Boomers on the verge of entering their elderly years. Overall, it finds that emerging senior populations break with those of the past, not only in terms of their size, but in their educational profiles, their household diversity, their greater gender equality, and their potential for economic inequality. These distinct social and demographic attributes will be magnified by the sheer size of the Boomer "age wave," which will transform state, regional, city and suburban populations in both growing and declining parts of the country.

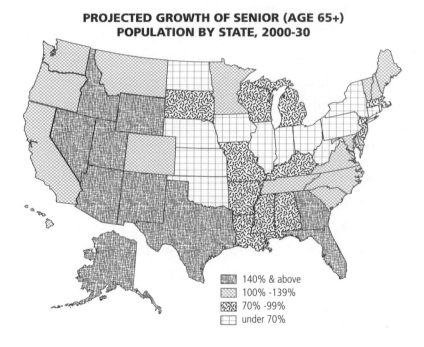

**PROJECTED GROWTH OF SENIOR (AGE 65+)
POPULATION BY STATE, 2000-30**

140% & above
100% -139%
70% -99%
under 70%

What are the local and regional ramifications of this impending transformation? With Boomer-dominated pre-senior populations now residing in metropolitan areas and suburbs of the South and West in large numbers, we can expect well-off "yuppie senior" populations to emerge in areas like Las Vegas, Denver, Dallas and Atlanta — places heretofore known primarily for their youthful profile. These populations may create demand for new types of housing and cultural amenities, and may continue to fuel the economic and civic growth of these areas as they remain involved in the labor force.

On the other hand, slow-growing metropolitan areas in the Northeast and Midwest will age as well, but more likely will be comprised disproportionately of "mature seniors" who are less well-off financially or health-wise. These populations may require greater social support, along with affordable private and institutional housing, and accessible healthcare providers. To the extent those resources are currently more focused on central cities, suburbs may need to play "catch-up," or cooperate more actively, with their urban neighbors to meet the needs of these aging-in-place populations.

The aging of existing Boomers will dwarf senior migration as a contributor to senior growth in all but a handful of retiree magnet areas, which many states and small communities aspire to become. Yet this dynamic creates enormous new market potential as seniors look to relocate to new neighborhoods or new homes within their existing communities. While most members of America's first "suburban generation" are not likely to select cities over suburban or small town areas as destinations, the sheer number of Boomers entering *seniorhood* indicates that even a small share of city-directed Boomers can have a positive population impact on cities. Those impacts could be economically valuable, too, if such movers are financially well-off and able to purchase homes in upscale neighborhoods, as the findings of the Brookings Institution survey imply.

Senior change across the nation's landscape over the next few decades will feature uneven but universal growth, and new challenges for all communities. Tracking the trajectory of these changes will be relatively straightforward for most places, because house-holds already residing there will provide the primary source of their senior growth. Public and private-sector leaders should thus be poised to evaluate how the impending explosion of both migrating and "homegrown" seniors shapes demand and, once again, trans-forms America's local economies, politics and societies in the first half of the 21st century. ⊚

THE UNBALANCING OF OUR HUMAN ECOLOGY

Peter Francese

The aging of our population is not happening uniformly across the nation. It is, in fact, happening far more rapidly in some states and regions than in others. This is occurring because some states have experienced higher than average out-migration of young adults combined with in-migration of retirees or those nearing retirement.

When a state or region's population ages more quickly than the nation, it can result in an "unbalancing of their human ecology." This means a demographic condition in which the number and rate of increase of retirees is not balanced by a sufficient number and growth of working age adults and children.

This can have significant economic and social consequences, because if this unbalancing persists in any part of the nation, it results in diminished workforce growth, increased out-migration of workers and a gradual decline in that area's overall economic activity.

One comparative measure of aging is the point at which half the population is younger and half is older, in other words: median age. For the United States, that age in mid-2008 was estimated by the Census Bureau to be 36.8 years. By comparison, that number was

Peter Francese is director of demographic forecasts for the New England Economic Partnership. He founded and served as publisher of *American Demographics* magazine, which became the nation's most authoritative resource on consumer trends. He is the author of numerous books, including *Marketing Insights to Help Your Business Grow*, and co-author of *Health Care Consumers* and *Communities & Consequences*, which is about the long-term implications of demographic trends in New Hampshire.

35.3 years at the time of the 2000 Census and 32.8 years at the 1990 Census.

This means that during the 1990s our nation's median age rose at an average annual rate of 0.25 years annually, but over the past eight years that rate has slowed a bit to under 0.20 years annually. During the past eight years (2000 to 2008), the U.S. population of ages 18 to 64 increased 9.4 percent, which was very close to the 10.8 percent increase for those ages 65 or older. The ratio of people between ages 18 and 64 to those ages 65 or older was approximately 5 to 1 in both 2000 and 2008.

With this viewpoint of the national picture of our aging population, consider the New England states. The table below shows the Census Bureau's estimate of median age for each New England state in 2008 and the Census figures for 1990 and 2000.

NEW ENGLAND STATE'S MEDIAN AGE 1990 TO 2008 AND RANK AMONG ALL STATES

	1990 Census		2000 Census		2008 estimate		Median age shift '90-'08
State	Median age	Rank	Median age	Rank	Median age	Rank	
ME	33.8	8th	38.6	3rd	42.0	1st	8.2 years
VT	32.9	25th	37.7	5th	41.2	2nd	8.3 years
NH	32.7	31st	37.1	8th	40.2	4th	7.5 years
CT	34.3	5th	37.4	7th	39.4	7th	5.1 years
RI	33.8	10th	36.7	10th	38.8	9th	5.0 years
MA	33.4	14th	36.5	12th	38.6	11th	5.2 years
US	32.8	—	35.3	—	36.8	—	4.0 years

New England states were six of the 12 oldest states in the nation in terms of median age in 2008, and all of those six states have aged far more rapidly than the nation over the past 18 years.

The obvious question is why has this region aged so much faster than the nation? For answers, we must look to the structure of its local governments — the vast majority of which are small and highly autonomous New England cities and towns. Counties, which are so important elsewhere in the nation, serve almost no purpose in New England.

The six New England states, for example, have about 14.3 million residents living in 67 counties. The state of Florida has about 18.5 million people, who coincidentally also live in 67 counties. But according to the Census Bureau, Florida has 95 school districts, between one and two per county, while New England has 700 to 1,300 school districts, depending on how they are counted, and between 10 and 20 per county.

It is very common for a small New England town with less than 10,000 residents to support an entire pre-kindergarten thru 12th-grade school system (plus a highway, fire and police department). So it should be no surprise that so many residents of these small places have to contend with high and rising property taxes — the vast majority of which go to pay for public schools.

Many town planning boards across the region have embraced the concept, that by reducing the percentage of housing units with children, a town can lower the number of children in public schools and therefore lower school-related property taxes.

While that concept is widely believed, it is completely devoid of any factual basis for the simple reason that almost all the costs of operating a school district are fixed costs and not materially affected by year-to-year changes in the number of students.

Nevertheless, towns across New England have often mandated age-restricted housing (that is, housing that can only be occupied by people ages 55 or older) as a way of controlling rising school-related costs. Part of the appeal is also the belief that occupants of age-restricted housing will pay their full property taxes, but make few, if any, demands on the town. That turns out to be another false assumption.

What occurs, in fact, are two types of cost shifting. The first cost shifting occurs when, after some lobbying by seniors, legislation is passed to relieve senior citizens of the burden of paying some or all of their property taxes. More than 100 towns in New Hampshire, for example, now provide property tax abatements to home owners ages 65 or older based on their income and assets.

Those tax abatements collectively shifted more than $20 million in property taxes to younger home owners last year in New Hampshire, up from less than $12 million in the 2000 fiscal year. Since 2000, the amount of those abatements has been increasing 10 percent per year, compounded annually. Coincidentally, approximately 4,000 units of age-restricted housing have been built in the Granite State since 2000.

The second type of cost shifting occurs in the price of health insurance. Any corporate, nonprofit or municipal employer in New England can attest to the fast-rising cost of health insurance. The main reason given is that hospitals and other healthcare providers are paid at below their costs by patients covered by Medicare or Medicaid. As the numbers of such patients rise, healthcare providers shift more of the cost of medical services to patients covered by private insurance.

Age-restricted housing is the only type of discrimination in housing that is permitted and it is widely used in many southern and western states. Age-restricted communities, designed specifically for retirees, have been a part of the housing landscape in Florida, Arizona and other snow-bird states for many decades.

The difference is that those states put almost no restrictions on the development of workforce housing for young families with children. So their human ecology has not been unbalancing in any significant way. By contrast, age-restricted housing in New England is seen as one of the legal tools (along with large lot zoning) that can be employed to limit, or exclude altogether, the number of affordable units attractive to young families with children.

The point is that when older people permit, and often eagerly support, discrimination in housing against younger people in order to exclude children from their towns, there are serious and very negative consequences. New England's future economic growth will be significantly impaired because so many young people have left the region, perhaps looking for a place that welcomes them rather than working so hard to exclude them.

Fifty years ago it was legal and even acceptable to keep people from buying a home in a town on the basis of their skin color or their religion. We as a society have come to believe that such discrimination was not only morally wrong, but bad economic policy. Not too many years from today, we may look back on the widespread age discrimination practiced in housing in New England and wonder why it took so long to recognize how damaging it was to the region's economy ... as well as to its soul.

The views expressed here are the author's alone and are not to be construed as those of the New England Economic Partnership. Portions of this essay appeared in an article by the author in Communities & Banking, *a publication of the Federal Reserve Bank of Boston. The author may be reached at peter@francese.com*

GOOD TO GRAY: OPTIMISM IS NOT A STRATEGY

Jeff Goldsmith

B oomers bring to the last decades of their lives a lot of positives: optimism, a sense of efficacy, curiosity, an intense work ethic, technological prowess, high education levels, and a high level of interest in health issues and in controlling decisions that affect their health. These are vital ingredients of a successful last third of life; they are self-generators of energy.

As difficult as it may be for Boomers to accept, we are not going to be able to control everything that happens to us in the latter phases of our lives. Merely hoping for the best, while ignoring the future consequences of decisions we postpone making today, is going to be an unsuccessful recipe for a happy aging process.

Eventually, aging is going to limit Boomers' options and possibilities. And, at a time and place not of our choosing, we will all die, however young we may feel today. In contrast to our accepting parents and grandparents, Boomers have been activists and have defined what they want to accomplish in every phase of their lives so far. Taking active steps that create options in the next 20 years will pay

Jeff Goldsmith is the president of Health Futures, Inc., and an associate professor of public health sciences at the University of Virginia. A University of Chicago-trained social scientist who has lectured at leading business schools in the United States, he has worked for both the governor of Illinois and the dean of medicine at the University of Chicago's Pritzker School of Medicine as a public policy analyst. For the past 25 years, he has served as a strategy consultant to both business and nonprofit enterprises. He is the author of *The Long Baby Boom* (copyright 2008, The Johns Hopkins University Press) from which portions of this article are reprinted by permission.

enormous dividends in life satisfaction, and renewed and strength-
ened relationships.

Americans should begin developing a culture and economy more
supportive of older people who wish to continue to work or contribute actively to their communities in other ways. We can also do a
much better job of anticipating and managing the health risks that
affect older Americans.

If we use our collective imaginations, we can design alternatives
to a stagnant, age-segregated society and interrupt the vicious cycle
of disengagement, deteriorating health and depression that can, all
too often, accompany aging. If we are imaginative, we can design
and reinforce an alternative, virtuous cycle: education and new
knowledge create new work roles and more active, engaged life,
which, in turn, generates positive health effects that enable people to
work and create longer, and generate the curiosity and energy to seek
more new knowledge. By reinforcing that virtuous cycle, we can postpone and spread out the social costs of the aging Baby Boom.

From a fiscal standpoint, new migrants to the United States and
the *echo* Boomers are like the cavalry riding to the rescue of our economy. Unlike our unfortunate colleagues in Europe, whose populations are declining and many of whose economies are stagnant,
Americans have had, until very recently, more robust and reliable
economic growth. Though we owe much more than we should to for-
eign governments because we have not saved enough publicly or privately, we have degrees of demographic and economic freedom
other societies do not have to solve our generational problems.

Whether our political system is flexible enough to permit these
changes is an open question. The bitterly polarized debate over healthcare reform yet again reveals fundamental ideological schisms in our
political system and a deepening mistrust of the political process by

the general population. A thoughtful response to the challenge of an aging Boomer Generation is not about markets, or entitlements, or generational equity, or preserving the New Deal. It is going to require greater candor and honesty than we saw in the healthcare reform debate. Specifically, we need to find the formula for a productive, growing and sustainable economy; a humane, vital society; and a constructive role of a huge, powerful generation born after World War II in that society.

Neither the glacial pace of demographic change, nor the seemingly glacial accretion of physical limitations related to aging, provides an immediate stimulus to action.

In a democracy, as Winston Churchill reminded us 80 years ago, we get the government we deserve. In a free society, we get the future we deserve. By denying the need to make conscious social and personal choices, we postpone the difficult decisions — for example, reallocating subsidies; increasing social and personal saving; increasing transparency and accountability for healthcare costs; and improving our own health. Neither the glacial pace of demographic change, nor the seemingly glacial accretion of physical limitations related to aging, provides an immediate stimulus to action.

In 2003 and 2004, AARP surveyed Boomers on their attitudes toward the future, and found a pervasive sense of optimism about their personal lives. The results sure look depressing from the cold light of late 2009: 67 percent of older Boomers and 80 percent of younger Boomers thought their lives would be better in five years, compared to only 37 percent of older Americans. Only 5 percent of older Boomers and 1 percent of younger Boomers thought their lives would be worse in five years.

More than two-thirds of those Boomers surveyed in 2003-2004 agreed with the statement, "What happens to me in the future mostly depends on me." It is clear that the brush with economic collapse experienced in 2008, and the lingering recession have sorely tested that optimism.

Now more than ever, what we Boomers need to do is to ask ourselves an important question: Given what we have witnessed of the end of our parents' and grandparents' lives, what would we do differently for ourselves? If we began working now to create different life paths, we can create degrees of freedom unimagined by our elders, lives we can be proud of and an end-of-life that we can accept with grace. ◉

THE THING ABOUT LIFE IS THAT ONE DAY YOU'LL BE DEAD

———— David Shields ————

A fetus doesn't sit passively in its mother's womb and wait to be fed. Its placenta aggressively sprouts blood vessels that invade its mother's tissues to extract nutrients. A mother and her unborn child engage in an unconscious struggle over the nutrients she will provide it. Pregnancy is, as the evolutionary biologist David Haig says, a tug of war: each side pulls hard; the flag tied to the middle of the rope barely moves. Existence is warfare.

Human beings have existed for 250,000 years; during that time, 90 billion individuals have lived and died. You're one of 6.5 billion people now on the planet, and 99.9 percent of your genes are the same as everyone else's. The difference is in the remaining 0.1 percent — one nucleotide base in every 1,000.

The Kogi Indians believe that when an infant begins life, it knows only three things: mother, night and water.

Francis Thompson wrote, "For we are born in other's pain, / And perish in our own." Edward Young wrote, "Our birth is nothing but our death begun." Francis Bacon: "What then remains, but that we

David Shields is the author of T*he Thing About Life Is That One Day You'll Be Dead* (from which this article is excerpted by permission of Knopf, a division of Random House, Inc. Copyright 2008 by David Shields). His eight previous books of fiction and nonfiction include *Black Planet, Remote, Dead Languages* and *Reality Hunger: A Manifesto*. A senior editor at *Conjunctions*, Shields has published essays and stories in *The New York Times Magazine, Harper's Magazine, The Yale Review, The Village Voice, Salon, State, McSweeney's* and *The Believer*. He is a professor in the English department at the University of Washington.

still should cry / Not to be born, or being born, to die?" The first sentence of Vladimir Nabokov's *Speak, Memory* is: "The cradle rocks above an abyss, and common sense tells us that our existence is but a brief crack of light between two eternities of darkness."

An infant breathes 40 to 60 times-a-minute; a 5-year-old, 24 to 26 times; an adolescent, 20 to 22 times; an adult (beginning at age 25), 16 times. Over the course of your life, you're likely to take about 850 million breaths.

Decline and Fall

If you could live forever in good health at a particular age, what age would you be? As people get older, their ideal age gets higher. For 18- to 24-year-olds, it's age 27; for 25- to 29-year-olds, it's 31; for 30- to 39-year-olds, it's 37; for 40- to 49-year-olds, it's 40; for 50- to 64-year-olds, it's 44; and for people over 64, it's 59.

Your IQ is highest between ages 18 and 25. Once your brain peaks in size — at age 25 — it starts shrinking, losing weight and filling with fluid.

Arteriosclerosis can begin as early as age 20.

As you age, your responses to stimuli of all kinds become slower and more inaccurate, especially in more complex tasks. From ages 20 to 60, your reaction time to noise slows 20 percent. At 60, you make more errors in verbal learning tasks. At 70, you will experience a decline in your ability to detect small changes, such as the movement of a clock hand.

Given a list of 24 words, an average 20-year-old remembers 14 of the words, a 40-year-old remembers 11, a 60-year-old remembers nine, and a 70-year-old remembers seven.

Most people reach skeletal maturity by their early 20s. At 30, you reach peak bone mass. Your bones are as dense and strong as they'll ever be. Human bones, with their astonishing blend of strength and flexibility, can withstand pressure of about 24,000 pounds per square inch—four times that of reinforced concrete—but if you were to remove the mineral deposits, what you would have left would be flexible enough to tie into knots. In your late 30s, you start losing more bone than you make. At first you lose bone slowly, 1 percent a year. The older you get, the more you lose.

There are now more people in the United States over 65 than ever before. Only 30 percent of people ages 75 to 84 report disabilities — the lowest percentage ever reported.

Five to 8 percent of people over 65 have dementia; half of those in their 80s have it. One of many dementias and the most common, Alzheimer's affects 1 in 10 Americans over 65, 1 in 2 people over 85.

At 68, Edmund Wilson said, "The knowledge that death is not so far away, that my mind and emotions and vitality will soon disappear like a puff of smoke, has the effect of making earthly affairs seem unimportant and human beings more and more ignoble. It is harder to take human life seriously, including one's own efforts and achievements and passions."

Aristotle described childhood as hot and moist, youth as hot and dry, and adulthood as cold and dry. He believed aging and death were caused by the body being transformed from one that was hot and moist to one that was cold and dry—a change which he viewed as not only inevitable but desirable.

About Life and Death

John Donne said, in a sermon, "We are all conceived in close prison, and then all our life is but a going out to the place of execution, of death. Nor was there any man seen to sleep in the cart between Newgate and Tyburn—between the prison and the place of execution, does any man sleep? But we sleep all the way; from the womb to the grave we are never thoroughly awake."

In 1900, 75 percent of people in the United States died before they reached age 65; now, 70 percent of people die after age 65. From 1900 to 1960, life expectancy for a 65-year-old American increased by 2.4 years; from 1960 to 1990, it increased 3 years. In England in 1815, life expectancy at birth was 39 years. In Europe during the Middle Ages, life expectancy at birth was 33 years, which is approximately the life expectancy now for people in the least developed countries.

Very old age in antiquity would still be very old age now. In the sixth century B.C., Pythagoras lived to be 91. Heraclitus of Ephesus died at 96. The Athenian orator Isocrates died at 98. The average life span has increased since the industrial revolution, but primarily because of declining rates of childhood mortality. In Sweden during the 1860s, the oldest age at death was usually around 106. In the 1990s, it was around 108.

In Europe during the Middle Ages, life expectancy at birth was 33 years, which is approximately the life expectancy now for people in the least developed countries.

In developed countries, one in 10,000 people lives beyond the age of 100. In the U.S., there were 37,000 centenarians in 1990; there are now around 70,000. The majority of American centenarians are female, white, widowed and institutionalized; were born in the United States of Western European ancestry; and have less than a ninth-grade education. Ninety percent of current American centenarians have an annual income of less than $5,000 (excluding food stamps, federal payments to nursing homes, and support from family and friends); they often say they were never able to afford to indulge in bad habits.

"Who wants to be a hundred?" asked Henry Miller, who died at 89. "What's the point of it? A short life and a merry one is far better than a long one sustained by fear, caution and perpetual medical surveillance."

Woody Allen, on the other hand, has said, "I don't want to achieve immortality through my work. I want to achieve immortality through not dying. I don't want to live on in the hearts of my countrymen. I would rather live on in my apartment."

The Gerontology Research Group — a loose organization of demographers, gerontologists and epidemiologists who study very old age — believes there's an invisible barrier at age 115. There are only 12 undisputed cases of people ever reaching 115. Very few people who reach age 114 reach 115; since 2001, a dozen 114-year-olds have died before turning 115. Right now there are, according to the GRG, 55 women and six men over age 110 worldwide. The oldest age ever reached was 122, in 1997, by a French woman. No matter how little you eat, how much you exercise, and how healthily you live, you apparently can't live longer than 125 years. In 5,000 years of recorded history, there's been no change in the maximum life span.

REASONS TO BELIEVE

REASONS TO BELIEVE

W hen a huge weather system approaches land from out in the ocean, the weather system creates waves in advance of its arrival. So it is with the aging of our population and our new longevity. The coming demographic shift is already stimulating creative responses, with viable concepts, models and programs proliferating. Those that effectively anticipate and respond to older adults' needs and wants will prosper. Others that appear promising today may fall by the wayside as the expectations of older adults and society in general evolve. The examples that follow are presented to stimulate thinking and encourage similar, actionable responses rather than to serve as endorsements of any specific program now in place.

Aging-in-Place

A 2007 national survey conducted by AARP showed that more than 80 percent of people over age 65 want to remain in their own homes, even if they need assistance in caring for themselves. Fortunately, innovations are available that can help meet this need, including home monitoring technologies, universal design for housing, more efficient delivery of home care, and even robots to provide care for homebound elders.

Home Monitoring Technologies

Home monitoring technologies are electronic devices that keep track of people at home, collecting health data or providing interventions on an emergency basis. The potential U.S. market for home monitoring technologies is vast and growing. On a global basis, it is estimated that up to one billion people suffer from chronic health conditions, and chronic care now consumes the vast bulk of healthcare spending. According to the National Alliance for Caregiving, there are about 19 million Americans caring for someone over the age of 75. There also is evidence that remote health monitoring can be an effective means for disease management and health promotion. Home monitoring technologies may prove attractive as traditional home care becomes too expensive.

Older people and their caregivers are increasingly open to using home monitoring technologies. The 2007 AARP survey found that three-fourths of older adults support the use of telemedicine to diagnose or monitor health conditions remotely in their home, and more than 90 percent support the use of telepharmacy to enable their doctor to keep track of their medications or send prescriptions to the pharmacy.

Major corporate players are now becoming interested in the home care marketplace. For example, in 2008, technology giant Intel entered the home monitoring marketplace with its own care management system, permitting healthcare professionals to monitor patients with chronic conditions while still at home. The new "Intel Health Guide" offers a touch-screen computer with video conferencing capabilities and a multimedia health education library for patients. This initial device is focused on specific disabilities — namely, congestive heart failure and chronic obstructive pulmonary disease. The device is not passive, but can actually initiate previously scheduled check-ups several times a day, collecting vital signs and sending information digitally to healthcare professionals.

Another home monitoring product, known as "QuietCare," is an embedded-in-the-environment device. QuietCare, developed by Living Independently Group, is now a product of GE Healthcare. The name "QuietCare" perfectly conveys the essence of the brand. QuietCare is similar to an alarm system, but instead of responding to an emergency event, like a fall, QuietCare instead silently monitors movement and uses a form of artificial intelligence to learn about individual behavior patterns. For example, the QuietCare system can indicate a possible bathroom fall by analyzing data from the activity sensors. If a person remains in the bathroom for more than one hour, the family caregiver or a monitoring office will receive an alert advising about the possibility of a fall.

GE's QuietCare, like Intel, promotes its product as a means of detecting potential risks and preventing adverse outcomes. It also aims to promote the idea of independence plus security, a combined message not always easy to maintain. Other companies are also developing new products and the marketplace is becoming crowded with age-adaptive brands that promise benefits to elders at risk: SeniorSafe@Home, iCare Health Monitoring, Philips Lifeline, Life Alert and Tunstall's wearable fall detector are only a few of the brands that will make the telehealth market grow in the future.

As a national resource and network, the Center for Aging Services Technologies is helping to expedite the development, evaluation and adoption of emerging technologies such as home monitoring and many other products and services that can improve the aging experience. CAST has become an international coalition of more than 400 technology companies, aging services organizations, research universities and government representatives.

To learn more, visit:

http://www.intel-healthguide.com/ihg.aspx?cid=GGLEIHG
http://www.gehealthcare.com/usen/telehealth/quietcare/
http://agingtech.org/index.aspx

Universal Design

To achieve the goal of remaining at home, homes themselves may need to be modified: indeed, 60 percent of all home remodeling already involves some kind of age-related modification. An even better approach might be to design housing initially in such a way that it would remain appropriate over the lifespan. That is the premise of Universal Design.

Universal Design is a creative approach to housing and living environments that aims to provide greater access for people with disabilities without stereotyping or stigmatizing them. For example, instead of installing a separate ramp to a building for those who are disabled, Universal Design aims for an environment that is accessible to all.

In housing for older adults, principles of Universal Design have stimulated many creative examples of age-irrelevant branding. For instance, the strategy of Universal Design has prompted the development of new types of shower grab bars and replacing toggle light switches with rocker-type switches that are easier to use. Universal Design elements can include zero-step entrances, location of the master bedroom on the ground floor and walk-in showers. Homes inspired by principles of Universal Design will have beneficial features affecting interior circulation; bathroom and kitchen design; home automation; and electrical switches and appliance controls, among other elements. These elements can have great appeal to older consumers. The call for "barrier-free," "accessible design" or "assistive technology" is likely to lead to significant product innovation in the aging society.

One example of such innovation is the Livable Design Home By Eskaton. Built in 2008 in Roseville, California, the project is the Northern California-based organization's practical and promotional approach to fast-forward the movement for older adults to live at home more comfortably, securely and affordably, for a longer period of time.

The Livable Design Home (formerly known as Eskaton National Demonstration Home) has been recognized by the National Association of Home Builders' 50+ Housing Council with its 2009 Gold Award for the "Best Detached Home in an Active Adult Community" and the AARP/NAHB "Livable Communities" award in 2010. It showcases universal, barrier-free design, and assistive technologies and energy efficiency — all in a real-world setting. The infrastructure can be incorporated into new homes, as well as retrofitted into existing homes. Moreover, the home is affordable for most people. Equal to the approximate cost of a few months in an assisted living community, upgrades with the amenities and services can enable older people to live many additional years in their own homes.

Livable Design By Eskaton was launched in 2009 to move the demonstration project to the next stage by providing developers, builders, designers, and building code and ordinance developers with guidelines to implement these proven-effective design innovations. Livable Design offers a certification program, which gives builders a unique marketing advantage and allows them to offer quality homes for aging-in-place. The Eskaton project is part of a growing interest among builders and developers to incorporate easy living, with sustainable and age-friendly construction in homes built today.

To learn more, contact:
Eskaton
5105 Manzanita Avenue, Carmichael, CA 95608
http://www.eskaton.org/

Franchising Homecare: Home Instead

Does anyone remember when doctors made house calls? "Nope, it's too expensive" is the typical response. Yet, one of the biggest obstacles to home care is also cost; it's often cheaper to move frail elders into a nursing home. But all surveys show that older people generally want to remain in their own homes. Could there be a market-based solution to the home care problem? What about a franchise for home care?

Home Instead Senior Care is a distinctive example of such a market-based solution, appealing to the same customer group that might be attracted to an assisted living or continuing care retirement community: people who need long-term care but don't want to go into a skilled nursing facility. Home Instead provides non-medical in-home care to older people. The ultimate customer, however, may be the adult child, the caregiver who faces daunting challenges.

The "Home Instead" name itself is an attractive one, making an implicit contrast with dreaded institutional care. Part of the challenge faced by customers is an emotional one: how to provide service and support for an aging parent in a way that protects dignity. With this point in mind, the market consulting firm Immersion Active recommended a more emotional approach to the Home Instead brand. Instead of focusing on "features and benefits," Home Instead offers taglines like "Remembering Grandma's Sunday Dinners." This more emotional approach produced a dramatic improvement in marketing and a bigger yield than the standard, informational approach to brand definition.

The lesson is clear: marketing home care demands more than just thinking about "problems-to-be-solved." A successful home care brand will make values and emotions a critical part of the messaging and positioning.

To learn more, contact:
Home Instead Senior Care
13323 California Street, Omaha, NE 68154
http://www.homeinstead.com/home.aspx

Robotics for an Aging Population

In science fiction movies from the 1950s, Japan often portrayed itself as a land of giant monsters. Today, the real Japan is becoming a robotic society; and population aging is a major reason for moving in this direction. More than 22 percent of the Japanese population is already above the age of 65 and that proportion will increase in the future. "With Japan's aging population, we need robots that can alleviate the burden of human tasks," says Toshihiko Morita, director of Fujitsu's Autonomous Systems Laboratory.

Those old sci-fi movies have already been replaced by a promotional film from a Japanese electronics company, Cyberdyne, showing an elderly patient with Parkinson's disease attached to a robot mechanism that provides artificial motion. This robotic suit could signal things to come. Today, there are robots exhibiting remarkable motor dexterity, such as the ability to unload a dishwasher. Interest in industrial robots on the assembly line dates back to the 1970s, when Japan took an early lead in the field. Today, Japan produces 70 percent of all the world's industrial robots, according to published reports.

Japanese investment in robotics has already led to significant achievements. For example, Panasonic has produced a robotic bed that can be transformed into a joystick-controlled wheelchair, responsive to a user's spoken command. In addition, there is a robot in the form of a giant teddy bear, called Riba, which can lift patients who weigh up to 130 pounds — a significant contribution for nursing home staff who need to move patients into or out of beds. Cyberdyne has also created a robotic suit, named "HAL" in recognition of the spaceship computer in the film "2001." HAL's development group received more than $5 million in support from the Japanese government.

The Japanese corporation, Speecys, is working on an Internet robot, designed to respond to verbal commands, much like the robots on the fictional "Enterprise" spaceship. The device, still under development, can read email out loud and surf the Web — big assets for those who are visually impaired. For older people with arthritis that impairs hand movements, voice activation could be a big plus.

Robots are not limited to physical tasks, but also include a "pet robot" named Paro, which provides companionship for isolated elders. Paro, which is the size of a large cat, was developed explicitly for those who are not able to care for living pets. In time, developers say, people forget that it's a robot and some relate to it almost as a baby. The positive response to Paro has not been limited to Japan. Residents in a retirement community in Virginia have been enjoying these robots since 2007.

Tim Hornyak, author of *Loving the Machine*, a book about Japan's robot world, has documented the prominent role of robots in Japanese popular culture. There are at least 20 companies in Japan now working actively in the elder care robot field. Government and industry often work together, which is a typical Japanese approach, to help researchers bring new products to the marketplace. While the United States continues to import nurses from the Philippines and elsewhere, the Japanese government has announced a plan to have "robot nurses" in place within a few years.

To learn more, visit:
http://www.lovingthemachine.com/

Livable Communities

It Takes a Village

We do not age in isolation, ideally, but in community. One creative response to that desire comes from Beacon Hill, an upscale historic district in Boston where neighbors have banded together to create a local community group that facilitates their interest to age in their own homes. Instead of long-term care, these Beacon Hill residents wanted a "concierge" service that maximized autonomy and the ability to make their own choices. In 2000, they launched "Beacon Hill Village," a nonprofit association to provide needed services — ranging from in-house health and social activities, to pet care, to computer support. Led by a core group of volunteers, these pioneers organized a system that has grown to an association with 400 members who pay annual dues, along with fees for "a la carte" services that are ordered as needed. They effectively "unbundled" services and payments to create a package that is less expensive than assisted living or conventional home care. This grassroots innovation has since been replicated in nearly 100 other locations across the country, including San Francisco, Denver, San Diego, Washington, D.C. and Falmouth, Massachusetts.

Beacon Hill Village tends to get the most publicity, but it was not the first effort of this kind. "Naturally occurring retirement communities" (or NORCs) were first recognized in the 1970s, appearing in urban high-rise apartment buildings, such as Manhattan's West Side. Like Beacon Hill, these NORCs included people who were aging-in-place and seeking government assistance to enable them to remain in their own homes. Since 1994, the state of New York has provided financing for social services, nursing and case management in places with high concentrations of older people, including some suburban neighborhoods, dubbed "horizontal NORCs."

In some respects, the emergence of NORCs was in response to declining federal funding for senior housing in the last decades of the 20th century. NORCs, along with grassroots initiatives like Beacon Hill Village, therefore, respond to a distinctive market segment: middle-class people who are not sick enough for Medicare, who have too much income for Medicaid services, and who are not rich enough for private individual care. But this segment is far from a niche, since it includes all but the very rich and the very poor.

Does the Beacon Hill Village model represent a wave of the future? Most efforts to replicate Beacon Hill have appeared in neighborhoods strong in "social capital," with residents who are well-connected and capable of leadership because of careers in professional work. The earliest NORCs also appeared in housing complexes with a tradition of organization inspired by labor unions or voluntary associations, along with government support. In short, innovations like Beacon Hill Village or NORCs do not "just happen" without substantial prior investment in either social capital or government support to sustain the systems that permit people to live independently.

To learn more, contact:
Beacon Hill Village
74 Joy Street, Boston, MA 02114
http://www.beaconhillvillage.org/

On Lok and the PACE Program
On Lok is a comprehensive health plan serving frail older people living in the San Francisco Bay Area. Its program of housing and supportive services offers an alternative of community based long-term care when nursing home care might otherwise prove necessary.

Originally based in San Francisco's Chinatown, the name "On Lok" means "place of peace and happiness" in Chinese and reflects the organization's mission and philosophy of care. On Lok currently operates five related nonprofit programs, including healthcare, housing and intergenerational programs. The largest and oldest of these is On Lok Senior Health Services, which provides quality, affordable care services for 950 frail elderly.

A key element of On Lok's success has been use of an interdisciplinary professional team to assess and develop individualized care plans. Their purpose is to encourage independence by providing services across the entire continuum of care: primary and specialty medical care, adult day healthcare, in-home health and personal care, social work services, and hospital and nursing home care.

On Lok has become the model for a national replication of its approach, known as the Program of All-Inclusive Care for the Elderly, authorized by the Federal Balanced Budget Act of 1997. PACE is a program of comprehensive health and social services for frail older persons, who would otherwise be eligible for skilled nursing care, but want to continue living at home. PACE offers comprehensive service delivery and integrated Medicare and Medicaid financing. The On Lok model, and its PACE replication on a national level, are an American version of a wider global trend toward integrated care. This is illustrated, for example, by Darlington in the United Kingdom and Rovereto and Vittorio Veneto in Italy, as well as "social health maintenance organizations" in the United States. These integrated care systems have common features such as a single entry point system, case management, geriatric assessment, reliance on a multidisciplinary team, and financial incentives to encourage flexibility and cost-containment.

To learn more, contact:

On Lok, Inc.

1333 Bush Street, San Francisco, CA 94109

http://www.onlok.org/Sharesite/content.asp?catid=240000335

Also, visit:

National PACE Association

801 North Fairfax Street, Alexandria, VA 22314

http://www.cms.hhs.gov/PACE/

Continuing Care Retirement Communities (CCRCs)

While most older people prefer to "age-in-place," there are those who seek housing for anticipated support needs that come with advancing age. Continuing Care Retirement Communities have been an important response.

The name itself tells the basic story: "continuing care." There are many variations on this theme, but generally communities offer residents the ability to move between independent living with services, assisted living, skilled nursing and memory care.

Customer resistance remains a challenge for CCRCs. A common refrain from qualified prospects is "I'm not ready for that yet." However, qualified prospects too often wait until they actually need skilled nursing before being "ready" to enter into a CCRC. The whole point of a CCRC is to provide what gerontologists refer to as a "continuum of care," enabling residents to move, as needs dictate, to various levels of care over time.

CCRCs represent an evolution of the modern retirement community. Though not embraced by those who want to age-in-place, this option fulfills an important market niche for age-segregated retirement living. It remains as appealing and viable today as when Sun City in Arizona, the first and still the most successful "modern retirement community," first opened its doors in 1960.

To learn more, visit:

http://www.aarp.org/families/housing_choices/other_options/

Also, visit:

http://www.aahsa.org/

Reinventing the Senior Center

Senior centers are a widely recognized program for older people. They were created because social workers and planners were concerned that elderly people lived in isolation and vulnerability; and that their needs could be met in congregate settings. The first senior center, the William Hodson Community Center, opened in the Bronx in 1943.

In time, the senior center model was reinforced by public policy. Since 1965, the Older Americans Act has provided support, offering service contracts for program activities. In 1972, the Act was amended to make senior centers the centerpiece of a national aging network. Today, there are an estimated 15,000 senior centers in the United States, serving as many as 10 million older Americans each year. Many of these centers receive funding under the Older Americans Act, offering a range of services — primarily nutrition, recreation and socialization. Although senior centers reach only a limited proportion of people over 65, they have established a solid place as an age-branded public service.

But senior centers might be in need of a makeover or at least "rebranding." Many older people feel that a local facility with services targeted to "old people" is the last place they want to be. More than two-thirds of center directors surveyed in 2005 by the National Institute for Senior Centers believed that Boomers, and those older, would simply not relate to being called "seniors."

How will *senior* centers reposition themselves to new generations of older people? One Pennsylvania facility actually changed its name to PEAK—People Experiencing Activity, Arts & Knowledge. In California, the Palo Alto Senior Center changed its name to "Avenidas." Phoenix, Arizona has reconfigured its 17 senior centers to move away from cafeteria-style meals and card-playing groups, replacing them with a "hip" new design that blends fitness centers, coffee shops and computer terminals.

The senior center of the future may have to base itself on a strategy of "successful aging." A still more radical strategy could be termed "organizational goal displacement." In other words, completely reframe the mission for an organization. The March of Dimes accomplished this. When the Salk vaccine cured polio in the 1950s, the March of Dimes lost its original purpose. But it successfully reinvented itself with a mission focused on birth defects, making necessary changes in order to remain relevant. Senior centers are likely to face such a challenge in years to come.

To learn more, contact:
National Institute of Senior Centers
NCOA
1901 L Street, NW, 4th Floor, Washington, D.C. 20036
http://www.ncoa.org/strengthening-community-organizations/

"Starbucks for Seniors"

In Chicago, one can find an alternative kind of senior center, a venue some have dubbed "Starbucks for Seniors." The officially named "LifeWay Café" is sponsored by the Evanston-based Mather Foundation. Recently Mather, which over the years has supported different kinds of senior housing in the Chicago metropolitan area, realized that older people in neighborhoods lacked access to places providing essential senior services. But instead of trying to build traditional senior centers, Mather took a completely different approach. They found storefronts that could be configured as coffee houses, and then added supplemental services, including learning centers, computer classes, fitness programs and other amenities. Instead of the traditional senior center, older people can find a new kind of gathering place, reflecting an active lifestyle in a familiar community setting. LifeWay Cafés are inspired by Starbucks more than by senior centers.

These LifeWay Cafés are typically located in downtown buildings that offer an accessible storefront. Patrons often say that these cafés feel more like coffeehouses than stereotypical senior centers, which is exactly what the planners had in mind.

A recent Environmental Protection Administration report on age-friendly communities noted: "You might see groups discussing books, sports, art or a concert; or getting help on a new computer program. Larger places may also have gyms, yoga and dance workshops, or educational classes in a learning center."

While developers for affluent retirement communities in rural areas have marketed their lifestyle as "a cruise in a cornfield," the LifeWay Café concept proves that it is not necessary to travel to a cornfield to find those amenities. It may only be necessary to reposition and rebrand senior centers. Inspired by successful commercial ventures, "Starbucks for Seniors" could be a sign of things to come.

To learn more, contact:
Mather LifeWays
1603 Orrington Avenue, Suite 1800, Evanston, IL 60201
http://www.matherlifeways.org/iyc_inyourcommunity.asp

Lifelong Learning

From Elderhostel to Exploritas

Elderhostel is a well-known educational travel organization, the largest in the world, aimed historically at older adults interested in lifelong learning. It currently offers 8,000 programs annually, in all 50 states and in more than 90 countries around the world. In 2009, Elderhostel changed its name to "Exploritas" and broadened its mission to appeal to adults of all ages.

The organization was founded in 1975 as an effort to provide later life learning in low-cost summer dormitory facilities. Elderhostel's basic form still includes programs that are typically six days long with three classes each day; and draws on subjects from the liberal arts. There are no tests, grades or other requirements of conventional education. International Elderhostel programs are longer, up to three weeks, and involve more travel.

Elderhostel's early growth was extraordinary, from 220 participants in 1975 to 20,000 five years later. By the year 2000, Elderhostel was enrolling more than 150,000 participants. The national and international networks, administered by a nonprofit organization headquartered in Boston, operate in many ways as a business enterprise based on a franchise model. Although they manage a vast travel network, liberal education remains the core of Elderhostel's mission. While no two programs are alike, all Elderhostel programs emphasize learning in a collegial environment, featuring lectures by experts combined with field trips for a more hands-on learning experience.

Elderhostel's recent change of marketing strategy reflects a recurrent challenge of how to make lifelong learning available without the negative stigma of age. Over the years, Elderhostel has changed its core program to respond to aging Boomers. In 2002, Elderhostel introduced a new sub-brand, "Road Scholar," which is available without age-restrictions. And the 2009 name change to Exploritas was a response to stagnating enrollments. Whatever form it takes, the organization has already proven that age is no barrier to learning.

To learn more, contact:
Exploritas
11 Avenue de Lafayette, Boston MA 02111
http://www.exploritas.org/

College-linked Retirement Communities

Many young people are anxious to leave campus life for the "real world." But in their later years, they may nurture nostalgic memories; and some even want to return to live near a college campus. A response to this growing desire is the emergence of college-linked retirement communities. Such communities are appealing to retirees who appreciate the intellectual and social atmosphere of a campus environment. Younger students benefit, too, from the intergenerational exchange and job opportunities working with older people.

College-linked retirement communities have now appeared in 50 towns with colleges, including Notre Dame, Dartmouth, Oberlin, Ithaca College, the University of Florida at Gainesville and the University of Michigan. These communities often appeal to people already affiliated with a school. For example, nearly seven out of 10 of the 200 residents at The Village at Penn State, an 80-acre retirement community that overlooks Beaver Stadium, are either alumni or retired faculty.

There is no single model for college-linked retirement communities. Some offer independent living while others are continuing care retirement communities, providing the full continuum of care. Costs are comparable to other upscale retirement communities, but feature the added benefit of lifelong learning.

Boston-based Campus Continuum solicits college alumni interested in retiring near their alma maters. Another college-linked retirement community is explicitly tied to those interested in football; while the Melrose Company, a builder of resort communities, is looking at golf communities near college campuses. The Hyatt Corporation operates its high-end "Classic Residence" in Palo Alto, California, on 22 acres leased from Stanford University.

Interest in college-linked retirement communities is bound to increase as retirement age hits Boomers, the best educated generation in history. All evidence points to prior education as the key predictor for interest in lifelong learning.

To learn more, visit:
http://www.bestguide-retirementcommunities.com/
http://www.campuscontinuum.com/

Osher Institutes for Lifelong Learning

In 2001, The Bernard Osher Foundation began considering support for lifelong learning programs aimed at older adults seeking personal fulfillment. The Osher Foundation was inspired by a number of successful models of older adult education, such as the 30-year-old Fromm Institute of Lifelong Learning at the University of San Francisco and the network of Institutes for Learning in Retirement, which had grown since the 1980s.

The Osher Foundation began making grants in 2002 for $100,000 a year for up to three years to colleges that would create new "Osher Lifelong Learning Institutes" (known as OLLIs). Today the foundation supports programs at 120 colleges around the country.

The Foundation's National Resource Center at the University of Southern Maine now provides technical assistance on educational programming for older people, as well as publications.

As the Osher Foundation's incentive for colleges to embrace the OLLI program, those that enroll 500 fee-paying members by the fourth year of operation become eligible for a $1 million endowment gift. If enrollment reaches 1,000, the college becomes eligible for an additional $1 million endowment gift.

There is wide variation in curriculum among the OLLIs, though certain elements are constant: non-credit offerings designed for adults aged 50 or over; a clear university connection and sustained university support; strong volunteer leadership and sound organizational structure; and a range of intellectually stimulating courses.

The OLLIs benefit from years of consistent branding, combined with — like Elderhostel/Exploritas — strong local initiative and variation. The success of the OLLI pattern resembles, in many ways, the "Universities of the Third Age," which have flourished in Europe. But the OLLI pattern also presents a distinctly American style and the Osher Institutes, in a short time, have proven to be a viable and impressive model for older adult education.

To learn more, contact:
The Bernard Osher Foundation
One Ferry Building, Suite 255, San Francisco, CA 94111
http://www.osherfoundation.org/index.php?olli

Also, visit:
http://www.usm.maine.edu/olli/national/

Financial Security

The New Swedish Pension System

Americans of all ages are recognizing the importance of private pension savings as a complement to Social Security. Some lessons may come from abroad, specifically from the New Swedish Pension System, introduced in 2000.

The New Swedish Pension System is a defined contribution plan that is both public and mandatory. The approach requires shared employee-employer contributions. Employees can choose from 650 mutual funds, with contributions invested collectively on behalf of employees. The Swedish government itself offers two stock funds, charging low fees comparable to index funds. Participants in all plans also have considerable flexibility in payout choices.

Experience with the New Swedish Pension System offers lessons about the strengths and limitations of any defined contribution pension system. The Swedish system is an add-on to a generous public pension provision, maintained in a country with a long commitment to social welfare. As with any stock investment plan, there inevitably are risks, which were evident after the bear market of 2001.

The new system provides participants with a wide range of choices. Yet recently more than 90 percent of new participants failed to make an active choice at all and opted instead for a government-sponsored default fund. The large number of options available can be paralyzing, which can be a problem in the United States with its more than 5,000 mutual funds.

The Swedish experience demonstrates that merely providing options does not lead to active choice and, as other experience confirms, investors do not always choose wisely. Consumer education on financial matters will be critical in the future.

To learn more, visit:

http://www.ap1.se/en/Our-mission/The-Swedish-pension-system/

Also, visit:

http://crr.bc.edu/images/stories/Briefs/ib_9-25.pdf

Long-term Care Insurance

Long-term care is a predictable risk for advanced age and it carries financial risk as well. The cost of a nursing home today can easily run above $75,000 per year. Up to 25 percent of people over the age of 65 will spend a period of time in a nursing home and up to 70 percent are likely to need some kind of long-term care services in their lifetime. Despite these risks, long-term care insurance remains a "hard sell." Consumers who have life insurance or fire insurance resist buying long-term care insurance — for a variety of reasons. As a result, the long-term care insurance field has a long history of problems and dashed expectations.

Why don't more people buy long-term care insurance? Some industry specialists say consumers mistakenly believe that long-term care insurance is too costly; but figures don't support this belief. Policies for people in their 50s are generally lower than automobile insurance. Many people, especially those in their 50s, say they are afraid they'll buy something they will never use.

Some resistance may also be based on misconceptions. Many people often do not understand their own insurance coverage, or they believe, mistakenly, that Medicare covers skilled nursing facility costs. Others who intend to shift assets in order to qualify for Medicaid may not be aware of recent legislative changes that make qualifying for Medicaid coverage much harder.

Long-term care insurance is a classic example of a financial product desperately in need of radical rebranding. As long as long-term care insurance is perceived by consumers to be "nursing home insurance," it remains a hard sell. Yet, as more people become aware of "longevity risk," it is possible that consumer attitudes toward long-term care insurance will shift.

In fact, the average age of long-term care insurance buyers has been falling steadily for more than 10 years and, in 2007, fell below 60 years old for the first time. There are now 8 million Americans who have some kind of long-term care insurance, and 46 percent of first-time buyers were in their 50s. Changes in national healthcare policies in 2010 and subsequent years may make long-term care insurance more available to wider groups in the population.

To learn more, visit:
http://crr.bc.edu/images/stories/Briefs/

Also, visit:
http://aahsa.org/article.aspx?id=1156

BenefitsCheckUp

Not everyone has a private pension plan or can afford to buy long-term care insurance. What about low-income elders who must depend on government benefits just to get by? How will they find their way to the benefits and services they need? Many older Americans, above all the poorest, are not receiving benefits to which they're entitled from current government programs.

A solution to this problem now exists. The "BenefitsCheckUp" system is the most comprehensive tool for helping older people gain access to needed benefits and services. BenefitsCheckUp is a computer-based screening service specifically designed to help older people with limited income and resources. It was developed over a period of years and is now administered by the National Council on Aging. Since 2001, millions of people have made use of BenefitsCheckUp.

The BenefitsCheckUp protocol now covers more than 1,800 public and private benefits programs available throughout the United States, including healthcare, prescription drugs, nutrition (including Food Stamps), energy assistance, legal services, in-home support services, tax relief, job opportunities and much more.

The BenefitsCheckUp process begins with identifying those benefits to which individuals are entitled — for example, enrolling Medicare recipients who qualify for "Extra Help" under Medicare's Part D (prescription drug coverage).

NCOA board member Warren Kantor has taken the BenefitsCheckUp methodology to a new level, helping low-income elders cut through red tape to access their entitled benefits. Kantor created the philanthropic Foundation to Benefit Our Seniors and later the Benefits Data Trust, designed to accomplish goals similar to BenefitsCheckUp. This new model was so successful that AARP, Kaiser Permanente, the Pennsylvania Department of Aging, the U.S. Centers for Medicare and Medicaid Services, and insurance giant United Healthcare have all contracted with Benefits Data Trust to find eligible recipients of their services.

To learn more, visit:
http://www.benefitscheckup.org/

Also, visit:
http://www.bdtrust.org/

Productive Aging

RetirementJobs

RetirementJobs.com is a leading career website for job-seekers in the 50-plus age group. Its website lists between 20,000 and 30,000 open positions, refreshed several times each week. Most openings are in the retail industry, but many are in financial services and other fields.

RetirementJobs.com was established in 2006 by executives with backgrounds in media, online recruiting and human capital management. Founder Tim Driver became convinced that the supply of older job seekers will soon be matched by a demand — due to a reversal in age bias in the workplace. He specifically noted that younger employees are likely to change jobs three times more often than older workers, and that older workers may have distinctive capacities to respond to an aging customer base.

RetirementJobs offers a website and job board listing thousands of job opportunities for experienced people seeking new employment. At first appearance, RetirementJobs is not much different from any other general-purpose job site, such as Monster or CareerBuilder. Yet its brand positioning reflects a distinctive mission and appeal to its niche audience, the 50-plus worker. Advice and stories on the website are focused on unique issues a mature worker is likely to encounter. For example, an article titled "Will a Job Affect My Social Security?" will be found on RetirementJobs. Most importantly, job seekers visiting the site know that employers posting jobs appreciate substantial work experience. RetirementJobs also administers a "Certified Age Friendly Employer" certification program, a designation earned by companies such as H&R Block, Borders Books, Marriott, Safeway, Staples and Manpower.

Other Web-based search companies focused on older workers include Workforce50.com and RetiredBrains.com, which both certify that employers listing jobs actually want to hire older workers. ExecSearches.com is targeted primarily at midlevel and executive positions in the government, health, nonprofit and education sectors. Even more distinctive is YourEncore.com, which targets experienced scientists, engineers and product developers seeking time-limited assignments.

To learn more, contact:
RetirementJobs.com, Inc.
204 Second Avenue, Waltham, MA 02451
http://www.retirementjobs.com/

Experience Corps

Experience Corps, created by the Civic Ventures group, is a volunteer network for Americans over the age of 55. The program is now operating in 19 major cities, including Boston, San Francisco, Minneapolis and Washington, D.C.

More than 2,000 Experience Corps members serve as tutors and mentors helping children learn to read. They work in urban public schools and after-school programs, where they help develop confidence for future success. Research shows that Experience Corps can boost student academic performance, help schools and youth-serving organizations become more successful, and strengthen ties between schools and surrounding neighborhoods.

Critical to the program's success, each Experience Corps member makes a substantial commitment, devoting a significant number of hours to tutoring and mentoring each week. Experience Corps members also receive rigorous training in early childhood education and literacy. And, Experience Corps members work in teams, developing supportive networks of colleagues.

Experience Corps projects place a critical mass of tutors and mentors at each school, so that the presence of the older adults changes the climate of the entire school. Experience Corps members also lead by example, engaging in the life of the school and community, thereby changing stereotyped images of aging.

Many volunteers take on leadership roles, helping set program direction in the schools where they serve.

In 2001, Experience Corps became part of the AmeriCorps network of national service programs and now is the largest AmeriCorps program engaging older adults.

To learn more, contact:
Experience Corps National Office
2120 L Street, NW, Suite 610, Washington, D.C. 20037
http://www.experiencecorps.org/index.cfm
Also, visit:
http://www.civicventures.org/

Healthy Aging

Successful Aging and Health Promotion

Health promotion and disease prevention are critical for positive longevity. The 20th century witnessed a major shift in the leading causes of death for all age groups, including older people, from infectious diseases and acute illnesses to chronic diseases and degenerative conditions. Americans are living longer, yet about 80 percent of older Americans are living with at least one chronic condition. In *The State of Aging and Health in America* (2007), the Centers for Disease Control and Prevention noted that three behaviors — poor diet, smoking and limited physical activity — were key risk factors for heart disease, cancer, stroke and diabetes. These were the basic causes of more than one-third of all U.S. deaths.

The National Institute on Aging recently analyzed epidemiological data about the health of aging Boomers and concluded that this group is likely to have lower health status later in life than preceding generations. Estimates of the future prevalence of obesity in the 60-plus population suggest an alarming "epidemic of obesity," which has been noted by leading public health authorities. According to the Centers for Disease Control and Prevention, 40 percent of adults ages 40 to 74 (54 million people), can be classified as pre-diabetic, a condition that raises the risk of developing Type 2 diabetes, heart disease or stroke.

There is an alternative to this disturbing scenario. The idea of "successful aging" is advanced by the landmark MacArthur Foundation study. The successful aging strategy encourages health promotion by psychosocial steps, such as improving behaviors around smoking, physical activity, diet, sleep and social networking, rather than through technological intervention. Above all, there is the importance of self-efficacy and a belief that positive health outcomes can be achieved by actions in one's personal control.

One group that has actively worked on behalf of health promotion is the Center for Healthy Aging, founded in Santa Monica, California, in 1976. In the decades since its founding, this private nonprofit agency has become a nationally recognized model for the delivery of healthcare focused on prevention of disease and education for a healthy lifestyle. The Center's clients age 55 and older range from those who are healthy and active to those who are homebound, frail, isolated and mentally ill. Renamed "Wise and Healthy Aging" in 2007, the Center provides health screening and education, as well as in-home support services such as friendly visiting, daily money management and care coordination. It offers community outreach programs, mental health services, day rehabilitation treatment and support groups for caregivers. Through all of these programs, the Center reaches more than 29,000 clients each year.

Healthy aging programs are expanding throughout the country. The Health Foundation of South Florida is now providing $7.5

million in grants to develop evidence-based health promotion programs through the Healthy Aging Regional Collaborative. This effort has produced 18 community-based projects focusing on chronic disease self-management, falls prevention, physical fitness and managing depression. In 2007, the Denver-based Colorado Trust launched a four-year initiative through its "Healthy Aging Initiative." This effort is now funding 20 groups managing senior-specific wellness programs, such as nutrition, exercise, disease screening and home modification. Programs like these in California, Florida and Colorado show a nationwide interest in making successful aging a new dimension of the longevity society of the future.

Can health promotion be more widely adopted? Can healthy aging reduce costs? Stanford University's Chronic Disease Self-Management Program, which began in 1992, is determined to answer these questions. The results are promising. Individuals who complete the Stanford Program have more energy, engage in more social activities and improve their communication with doctors. Most significantly, perhaps, they develop a stronger sense of self-efficacy and empowerment. Published research shows cost savings also arising from chronic disease self-management. The program was adopted nationally by Kaiser Permanente in 1998.

To learn more, contact:
WISE & Healthy Aging Headquarters
1527 4th Street, 2nd Floor, Santa Monica, CA 90401
http://www.wiseandhealthyaging.org/cms/home.html

Also, visit:
Stanford Chronic Disease Self-Management Program
http://patienteducation.stanford.edu/programs/cdsmp.html

Eden Alternative and Green House Project

The Eden Alternative is making a dramatic attempt to change the meaning of long-term care and to make healthy aging a part of the later stage of life. The Eden Alternative began as an experiment in a rural skilled nursing facility in upstate New York in 1991. William Thomas, M.D., a geriatrician at the Chase Memorial Nursing Home, had a goal to decrease the plague of loneliness, helplessness and boredom found in nursing homes. He set out to create a unique, more enjoyable environment, which featured a habitat containing birds, dogs, cats, rabbits and a flock of hens, along with indoor plants and gardens of flowers and vegetables. To the pleasure of residents, he also scheduled regular visits and activities to bring children into the facility. A decade and a half later, through a "Pioneer Network," the Eden Alternative has become a national and international movement of "culture change" in nursing facilities and other long-term care communities.

The Eden Alternative is the most prominent and visionary endeavor to promote humanistic culture change in long-term care. Others of note in the United States include the Wellspring model and the Live Oak regenerative community. Initiatives have been introduced in Australia, Canada and Switzerland as well. And the United Kingdom is home to the "person-centered approach" to the dementia care effort pioneered by the Bradford Dementia Group.

How far can the Eden approach go in transforming the culture of long-term care facilities? Adopting the Eden label is one thing; but changing a facility's culture is another. In recent years, the Eden approach has been extended to refashion long-term care in smaller community settings. Notably, there is the Green House project. Instead of a full-scale nursing home, the Green House project develops small, family-size homes for six to eight residents, supported by paid caregivers who work six hours per day and also serve as homemakers and friends. The Green House, with its "warm, smart and green" approach, is a small intentional community. In effect, it de-institutionalizes long-term care and returns it to a more human scale. Whether in an *Edenized* facility or in a Green House, this new vision of long-term care represents an affirmative and visionary approach to healthy aging.

To learn more, contact:
Eden Alternative
14500 RR 12, Suite 2, Wimberley, TX 78676
http://www.edenalt.org/

Cognitive Fitness
The hope for "cognitive fitness" grows out of a belief that brain health and cognitive vitality may lie within our power. This hope was encouraged by the pioneering work of Dr. Marian C. Diamond, who promoted the concept of "neuroplasticity," demonstrating that the brain can, in effect, "rewire itself" to compensate for losses. Since the 1960s, Diamond has developed the implications of neuroplasticity for brain health and performance in later life.

One of the biggest fears of aging Boomers is the specter of cognitive impairment. Today, there is a rapidly growing interest in natural, non-drug-based interventions to keep our brains sharp as we age. For example, the Japanese company Nintendo has marketed cognitive fitness games, such as Brain Age and Brain Training, shipping over 15 million of these units worldwide since 2005. The Nintendo product, developed by one of Japan's leading neuroscience researchers, Dr. Ryuta Kawashima, asks gamers "How old is your brain?" and promises to "train your brain in minutes a day" with a fun, rewarding form of entertainment." In the U.S., Posit Science introduced the idea of "brain exercise."

A similar product, the Dakim Brain Fitness system, is the result of six years of development in consultation with top senior care providers and brain health researchers, inspired by studies indicating that regular cognitive stimulation can help fight memory loss and related ailments. Each Dakim Brain Fitness unit presents thousands of games, puzzles and other brain-building activities on a user-friendly 17-inch touch screen appliance. Exercises range from anagrams and name-that-tune challenges to TV-style scenes and narrated literary passages complete with special effects that include follow-up questions requiring use of short-term memory and deductive reasoning.

Current research is likely to create new approaches to cognitive fitness in the future. For example, a team at the University of Illinois is looking at non-invasive interventions such as aerobics training and computerized cognitive training. Researchers at the Institute for Creative Technologies at the University of Southern California are applying virtual reality methods to assess and enhance neurocognitive functions. The Oregon Health Science University is investigating the use of gaming tools for real-time cognitive monitoring to help older persons remain independent, active and productive.

To learn more, visit:
http://www.positscience.com/contact.php
http://www.brainage.com/launch/index.jsp
http://www.dakim.com/

Public Outreach: "Aging is an Active Verb"
Television stations across California received Aging Services of California's new public service announcements — and began airing

the 30-second spots immediately and regularly. It seemed that the nonprofit organization's inspiring campaign message — "Aging is an *Active* Verb" — resonated with many stations' public service directors, who selected the *pro-aging* spots from the hundreds of PSAs submitted every month. Several new series and three years since its launch, the campaign continues to earn regular placements and millions of viewer impressions.

The goal of the campaign and the TV spots, specifically, is to redefine "aging" as an all-inclusive, active process rather than a label placed on the old and frail. The ads declare "Aging is just a number" and feature a wide range of prominent individuals who accomplished great things later in life. Among those profiled are blues legend "B.B. King — still touring the country at 82"; "Ansel Adams — photographed Yosemite at 81"; "Celia Cruz — earned her third Latin Grammy at 76"; and "John Glenn — returned to space at 77." To complement these high-profile achievers, the spots also feature *regular* folks such as "Duane — golfed his age at 77"; "Marjory — advocates for seniors at 81"; and "Stan — swims a mile a day at 83"; among others. The Emmy-nominated PSAs were the creative work of Pilotfish Productions (www.pilotfish.tv), which has gone on to reproduce the spots for a number of other states.

Print announcements, articles, online use by Aging Services' members, even promotional gear round out the campaign's far-reaching communications platform.

To learn more, contact:
Aging Services of California
1315 I Street, Suite 100, Sacramento, CA 95814
http://www.aging.org/